Escaping the Lyme Inferno

Memoirs of Lyme Disease and other Medical Miseries

Edited by Eric Karlan

ISBN: 1519162642
ISBN-13: 978-1519162649

Printed by CreateSpace, An Amazon.com Company

DISCLAIMER

This book contains general information for educational purposes only. The information provided in this book does not constitute medical advice, and is not meant to be used, nor should it be used, to diagnose or treat any medical condition. For diagnosis or treatment of any medical problem, consult your own physician. NEVER DISREGARD PROFESSIONAL ADVICE OR DELAY SEEKING MEDICAL TREATMENT BECAUSE OF SOMETHING YOU HAVE READ IN THIS BOOK. The publisher, editor, and authors are not responsible for any specific health or allergy needs that may require medical supervision and are not liable for any damages or negative consequences from any treatment, action, application or preparation, to any person reading or following the information in this book. References are provided for informational purposes only and do not constitute endorsement of any websites or other sources.

The names of the authors and other figures in this collection of stories have been changed in order to protect their identities and privacy.

CONTENTS

DEDICATION

This book is dedicated to Doug

Unknowingly, your personal journey through unchartered waters to save your family has saved the families of those in this book and countless others. We are humbled and inspired by your intellectual curiosity, ingenuity, and pioneering spirit.

You unselfishly shared your experience. Gratitude and appreciation do not begin to express the recognition you deserve.

PROLOGUE

In every war there are select groups of people who form resistance movements – those people who challenge authority, question the experts, and use their collective intelligence to defeat the enemy. Some of these people risk their lives to save others, as well as themselves.

Our lead character Sage found herself in this war ten years ago. A war against a disease and a war against the mainstream medical community. As in any war, one develops bonds and relationships with other people fighting the same battles. This book is a collection of their stories - their tragic memoirs of escaping the Lyme inferno.

These people - along with countless others - shared resources, information and intuitions. These otherwise strangers united in this war, forming an underground healing community that thrived on innovation, experimentation, and determination. A courageous group of individuals who some days survived only on the respect, compassion, and support of others they would never meet in person.

This book is not about tick-borne illnesses. It is about the isolating and lonely journey to eradicate the infections caused by them. While these infections can wreak havoc on the human body in a myriad of ways, they are rarely identified, diagnosed, or treated properly. Lyme and tick-borne diseases can manifest in anything from acute psychiatric disorders, to neurological horrors, to cardiac malfunctions and muscular-skeletal issues. And that is just naming a few.

Every person in this book had experiences as unique as fingerprints. Yet their stories are the same in so many ways.

This is why I was compelled to edit this collection of memoirs. To share these people's experiences so that others can find themselves in these stories. This book is not and cannot be a medical manual. But it can be a sanctuary - an unlikely source of comfort, a reassurance that you are not alone, an inspiration to keep on fighting.

Maybe you have been told you are crazy. Maybe you have endured undiagnosed ailments for years with no relief or solution. Maybe you are prescribed to an endless regimen of drugs just to survive the day - let alone make progress healing. Maybe you have a loved one who is suffering and nobody has an answer.

If you are one of these people, then this book is for you.

This is not a book of medical advice. This is a collection of memoirs – of desperation and unimaginable suffering, and of people who took personal responsibility for their wellbeing. These people had unwavering commitments and desires to be healed. Truly healed. These people did not just want to FEEL better. They wanted to BE better. To be whole. To be healthy. And they have refused to settle for less.

CALL ME SAGE

There is no way to know whether I could endure the ordeal of reclaiming my health again. It was an all-consuming traumatic and draining disaster with far reaching consequences – physical, emotional and financial. Writing about it, or even speaking about it, feels insufficient, for there is no accurate way to reenact the horror of having to save my own life in a country that boasts the most advanced and sophisticated medical system in the world – a medical system that both refuses and denies to acknowledge one of the most debilitating epidemics of our time: Tick-Borne Diseases, particularly Lyme disease.

I was vaguely aware of a shift in our medical establishment over the years of emerging managed care, but now I was certain that the days of TV's Dr. Marcus Welby had disappeared for good. Instead of having someone listen to your ailments while viewing the body as a whole while trying to discern the etiology of the complaints, patients now get churned in and out of physicians' offices at breakneck speed. You usually end up spending more time filling out privacy forms and answering insurance questions than speaking to an actual physician. Then, faster than the high-speed Acela train, you are usually propelled to a specialist who ONLY handles your particular symptoms, or to the pharmacy for some quick-fix drug. You know the drugs –

the ones we see on television each day where twenty-five of the thirty seconds of the commercial describes the fifty dangerous side effects that could easily put you in the hospital, give you a new disease, or possibly kill you.

As a woman in my late forties I was facing a medical system of prescription-writing internists and specialists all trained to manage symptoms. There was no one trying to connect the dots and examine the big picture when all of a sudden my healthy body deteriorated into a state of physical and emotional chaos, malfunction, pain – a life-altering nightmare where hell sounded like a vacation in paradise.

I had always thought I was born with a strong physical constitution. While my childhood was filled with upheaval, instability, and emotional suffering, my body was vibrant, resilient, and seemingly healthy. On some level I knew I relied on this health and strength in order to cope with a home life that made the movie Mommie Dearest look like a Saturday morning cartoon. The silver lining in this firestorm was that I learned early on that trusting authority, or anyone close to you, can often end up with catastrophic results. This acute sense of intuition was crucial to my survival. Had I been a happy, loved, nurtured, and trusting soul when I was younger, I would have likely ended up dead when this debilitating physical illness struck with ferocity in adulthood.

Despite the train wreck of my early life, I had always been surrounded by kind, compassionate, intelligent, and successful physicians. Growing up in a medical community (my father and all our family friends were doctors, dentists, specialists, you name it) you learn that these people are regular people, not overpaid rich gods like the masses perceive. Most were decent human beings, hardworking and earnest in their desire to reflect well on their profession. This knowledge was my safe zone in a crazy universe and while it sometimes seemed that these doctors could be a tad full of themselves, I basically trusted them in my own limited way. This limited but viable trust, however, would be later detonated and blown to smithereens when I got seriously ill. Isn't that ironic? The people I trusted the most for decades ended up being completely deficient and practically useless to me when it came to my life-threatening disease, not because they were bad people, but because they were inadequate healers.

I had never forgotten the night I viewed an award-winning documentary about the Lodz Ghetto during the Holocaust. Lodz was a harrowing historical event; I believe less than a 1,000 people survived out of almost 250,000. I was stunned that any survived at all and awed by those left standing and breathing. One of the people who watched the film that night was a bright and accomplished psychotherapist. When I asked him how those few people survived, he did not hesitate for a second: "They all had a basic mistrust of authority." His certainty and clarity about this was branded in my head that night and I always knew it could be a touchstone of sorts to ensure my own wellbeing someday. Maybe there was some providence in that evening that impacted my decisions to challenge the establishment some twenty years later.

Fast forward...

I was forty-seven years old. Had a husband and children I adored. Life was good. There were normal modern family stresses. But life was good. I felt blessed. I looked great – had vitality, energy, and purpose. All systems were "go" to enjoy my adulthood. I was happy and grateful. Little did I know that the utter torment I endured in childhood was just a dress rehearsal for the mother lode of cataclysmic realities that arrived at age forty-seven. While there is not a single, happy memory I have of my childhood, those horrible days looked Utopian compared to what happened when my body failed me.

My journey into the depths of hell all began when I awoke one morning with acute stomach pains. My body felt foreign. I thought immediately: "Something is very wrong." My literal and figurative gut set off an alarm in my head. This was trouble. Off to the emergency room I went. Little did I know that this was the beginning of a long and intimate relationship with emergency rooms and walk-in clinics. My nightmare had begun.

The emergency room doctors could not find anything wrong, so they sent me to my internist – a top-notch, hotshot, A-list doctor with a closed practice. I had always liked him. His peers thought he was a genius; every doctor in town used him as their doctor. He was Ivy League educated. People were enthralled with him; I was not. I was Ivy League educated, too. "Big deal," I thought. Still, he was normally nice – but then again, I was normally healthy and normal had just gone the way of the dinosaur. He outsourced me to a gastroenterologist. This one seemed like a smart guy, a nice guy. He appeared to be well respected. He ran many tests: blood work, colonoscopy, endoscopy. Terms like "irritable bowel" and "leaky gut" were thrown out. (I just love the terms they throw out when they have no clue why you are in pain.) I had always had a cast iron stomach. My intuition said he was wrong, but I chose to trust him.

Big mistake.

Within weeks of this initial episode, a horrible feeling of anxiety and panic took over my body. It was scary bad. Beyond words. I reached out to a therapist because my emotions made no sense to me. I was happier than ever – so then why did I feel like I was having a nervous breakdown? Then more physical pain got layered in. I started having excruciating body pain. My neck, back, and muscles all over. My thigh muscles burned. The pain was so bad that I could not roll over in bed. Insomnia set in, too. I was a person who loved my sleep and now, all of a sudden, sleeping two hours was my limit. For the first time, I understood how sleep deprivation could be used as torture. My therapist said it was amazing and miraculous that I survived my childhood and went on to attribute these events as the post-traumatic stress that needed to escape my body. My intuition said there was something more but I chose to believe her.

Another big mistake.

To make matters worse, I started getting black and blue marks all over my arms and legs. Then the chest pain set in. I also started to have neuropathic sensations throughout my body. My fingers in my left hand had tremors. I could not hold my left arm out straight. My arms and legs were constantly tingling and I had numbness in my toes. Without warning, cramping would freeze my toes in various unnatural directions. It was excruciating. Not to mention the unrelenting sciatica.

Over the next several months, more and more symptoms crept in. I had bladder pain from hell. So many OB/GYN symptoms set in that I had to have a hysterectomy. There were mysterious cuts in my private areas. I developed mouth sores. I had double imaging and blurry vision, headaches and crushing ear pain. My hair was even starting to fall out in clumps in the shower and on my hairbrush. I cried incessantly. I could not swallow on my left side. In fact my whole left side felt like I had had a stroke. My legs began to fail me. I used to walk four miles a day. Now I could barely stand without holding on to something. I was so terrified of never being able to walk again that every single morning I crawled (literally) to the treadmill, pulled myself up, and clutched the handlebars for support to walk for as many minutes as my body could bear each day. I was afraid that, like a shark dies if it stops swimming, I would die if I stopped walking.

The bottoms of my feet felt like I was always stepping on cracked glass. I was losing control over every part of my body. I was shivering all the time, freezing cold, unable to warm up. My head seemed like it was split in half by a meat cleaver. The left side felt disconnected from the right - like someone took a permanent marker and drew a line directly down the center of my head. The left side had constant static and crackling. I was reminded of frying marbles as a child. My marbles were definitely fried - but only on the left side. Weird. The right side felt perfectly normal. The left side of my face had the sensation of being rearranged and distorted. Each time I went to a mirror I expected to see something that resembled a Picasso geometric portrait. The shoulder pain on my left side brought me to my knees. Exploding black floaters went off in my left eye like fireworks. I experienced such bad dry eye that it felt like my eyeball was torn up.

I plunged into despair and terror. My body was twitching constantly. I had so many fasciculations - muscle twitches, especially in my legs - that I felt like I was an ongoing package of jiffy pop. The popping was relentless. My sinuses were clogged intermittently, and my jaw and teeth had weird sensations. My skin took on a lizard-like dryness, like it had aged ten years in a few months. And breast pain - horrible tenderness and soreness. Not to mention the feeling of electrical currents in my arms. Every body system was shutting down on me.

One night my entire spinal cord felt like it shorted out. Shattered into fragments like someone had thrown me into an electrical socket. I felt literally fried that night. Things got really scary after that. My entire central nervous system had simply caved in that single moment.

My vaginal tissue was so inflamed and painful that I used to fill condoms with crushed ice and insert them to get some relief from the constant burning. The hot-shot doctor said it was yeast. They were wrong. They were always wrong.

My throat was constantly burning and inflamed, too. The tonsils were a mess. I was always having my husband check all my body parts with a flashlight. I was insane with the migrating and unrelenting ailments.

It seemed like a cruel irony that I could no longer tolerate a sunny day because of acute light sensitivity. The sunlight felt like it was branding my eyeballs. I craved clouds. And I had debilitating sound sensitivity, too. Gone were the days of cranking up the radio in the car to sing along. Now my drives needed to be silent. At home, I kept walking around the house telling everyone to turn the TVs down - that everything was too loud, uncomfortably loud. Everyone looked at me confused. No one else could hear what I could hear.

My older son was a senior in high school and had just been accepted early decision to his desired college. He wanted to show me the campus, which I had never visited. Tough to drive three hours and walk around a campus all day when you can barely get out of bed in the morning. Impossible really. But I wanted to deliver for him. The three-hour car ride was difficult for me. I remember feeling jumpy and weepy. While walking around the campus, trying to be cheerful and excited for him as he proudly showed us points of interest, I lost complete feeling in my foot. I went hysterical. Completely freaked out. We went into a building and I ripped my boot off and tried to get feeling back in the foot. It was terrifying and I will never forget the trauma of that moment and the dread that I would likely never see my son as a student there, let alone graduate, because I would likely be dead before he finished his high school year if things continued to spiral downhill.

On another occasion, my younger son was ill one evening and called for me at 2:00 in the morning. His bedroom was on an upper floor and I remember feeling like I was climbing Mount Everest to reach him. How could I not be a mother to him? He was calling me. I was scared. If I got any sicker, would I have to abandon all parental responsibilities, even the most fundamental ones? How would my children not feel abandoned by me? I was creeped out beyond belief by these thoughts.

I felt like a Mexican jumping bean, experiencing ADHD symptoms. This was highly unusual for me. Normally, I could sit for hours and read a book or do a puzzle without moving. Not anymore. I felt like I was literally jumping out of my skin. Could not even sit still at the dinner table when I was able to get there. Concentration went right out the window. Instead of devouring classic novels, I was barely able to skim People Magazine. Each paragraph had to be reread several times before any content was absorbed.

Hospitals were a home away from home for me. I was so thankful for emergency rooms physicians. Not sure why the ER doctors are less arrogant than private practice – maybe because private practice doctors get the personal adoration of their patients who blindly trust them to medicate them into numbness. ER doctors do not cultivate those enslaved relationships. They deal in crisis mode. Gotta love those guys. Walk-in clinics rock, too. Instead of writhing in pain, wondering if you are having a heart attack while the hotshot A-listers take eight hours to call you back, you can go to a walk-in clinic, have an EKG, and be home before the A-listers get back to you – only to tell you that the first available appointment is three days away. Gotta love those walk-in clinics.

Between these visits to walk-in clinics – the only medical visits that kept me going – I spent my days going from my Harvard-educated "top notch" doctor to every -ologist he could outsource me to. Within four months, I had been examined by a cardiologist, gastroenterologist, gynecologist, physiatrist, psychologist, neurologist, urologist, radiologist, dermatologist, ear, nose and throat specialists, acupuncturist, chiropractor, periodontist, optometrist, and ophthalmologist. No one had any answers. They all wanted to medicate me with anxiety drugs. They blamed perimenopause. Can you imagine? If every woman underwent what I endured as a normal part of "the life change," there would be no females living over the age of fifty; they all would have killed themselves. The suffering was unimaginable. I could not walk or drive. I could barely move out of bed. Trips out of the house were limited to medical appointments and still I got no answers. I just could not wrap my brain around how all these top-notch doctors could say I was fine. They all seemed like Pinocchio at this point. In my mind I kept saying, "Tell me another lie, why don't you!"

I begged my husband to check me into a hospital where they could figure out what was happening, and at one point he even started to look at me like I was insane. He believed the doctors even when I told him I was dying. I KNEW that I was dying. On a scale of one to ten, the pain was at least a twenty on most days. My crying jags persisted daily. Friends started to pull away from me. They thought I was going insane. Much later I realized this was a renewed life lesson: when you are needy, people run for the hills. When you are strong and full of vitality, people cling to you like barnacles.

So my team of A-list physicians had no clue what could be causing my ongoing misery. Yet my intuition was screaming at me, insisting that all my ailments were linked. After months of appointments, I had made a list of each session and each symptom, trying to connect the dots. Yet, when I presented my Harvard hotshot with these notes and my theory, he dismissed the idea. "Put your notes away," he said. "Today we are focusing only on your chest pain."

In this instant, Dr. Hotshot became an asshole forever to me. I had known this guy for twenty-five years. He knew I was not a hypochondriac because I was never sick for twenty-four of those twenty-five years. I had nightmares about him for years after this.

I lived in Connecticut, in the woods, on acres of land where the deer lived outside my front door. This is "ground zero" for Lyme and tick-borne diseases, yet not a single practitioner ever considered this to be the underlying etiology. None of them, with their reams of blood work orders ever considered to test for Lyme disease and the most common co-infections: Bartonella, Babesia and Ehrlichiosis/Anaplasmosis. How is it possible that kids in Connecticut go for yearly pediatric visits and get tested for tuberculosis religiously, but no one thinks to test kids for Lyme disease when they are constantly playing outside in the woods, parks, and playgrounds. They participate in scouts and go to camps. Now that is nuts and insane. Does a six year old child in Connecticut have a better chance of getting Lyme disease or TB? Idiots.

It turns out that Lyme disease is exactly what set this inferno off in my body. Lyme was first mentioned to me by a couple of friends who were infected and while they had not crashed and burned like I had, they seemed convinced I had it, too. I thought I had something more deadly and fatal. At that point in time, I was unaware that tick-borne illnesses can trigger many deadly manifestations. Much like Lyme disease's closest relative Syphilis, it can mimic and present as many other illnesses. (A doctor at a meeting I attended called Lyme "the bigger and badder cousin of Syphilis.") The neurological manifestations and symptoms are particularly menacing and the psychiatric ones are of course nightmares.

Recollections of a November 2003 Newsweek article on diseases of the mind resurfaced. I remembered they wrote about Lyme disease and syphilis. And I remembered one line in particular: "When penicillin was first used to treat syphilis, thousands of cured schizophrenics were released from mental asylums." I could believe it.

My condescending top-notch internist told me that Lyme disease did NOT present as my symptoms. Overall, I had at least forty Lyme symptoms. The neurologist, to his credit, said I might have Lyme, but the urologist thought I might have multiple sclerosis. Everyone else thought I was just nuts.

I was truly considering suicide as a way out of the pain. My trust in the medical establishment was destroyed. My hope for ever feeling normal again was shattered. I lay in bed all day and each sleepless night trying to figure out how to kill myself without hurting my children. Gas? Pills? Razor? I decided against it. There is no way, I thought, you can kill yourself without damaging your children forever.

What about prayer? Prayer? Prayer seemed to help many others. But for me – I do not think so. G-d and I had some communication issues. He was not in the habit of hearing me so I had stopped reaching out to him years before. I think G-d's vacation schedule needs to be cut back a bit. Just my opinion.

ONWARD.

I had run out of allopathic physicians at this point. Losers. So I began to entertain the unthinkable: ALTERNATIVE MEDICINE. These were the very people I was always told were quacks. But desperation had set in. This option had to be better than suicide. If the school janitor could have helped me at this point, I was open to it. Did I mention how desperate I was?

Well, it turns out that these "quacks" actually look at the body holistically. They are trained to think and practice that body parts and symptoms are actually connected. So I packed up and left my academic, snooty, Ivy League background and was now on the hunt for a "voodoo guru" someone, anyone who could stop my runaway train to the morgue.

Did I mention how utterly alone and isolated I felt? You have no idea what alone is until you get sick and crazy and start challenging the medical establishment. Not only did everything I once thought to be true and real get pulled out from under me, but now I had to explore unknown territory and I had no one to help me navigate. Everything I had once mocked, dismissed, or scorned was now on the table.

A naturopath was the first alternative doctor I saw. I did not even recognize myself at this point. Where did my confidence go? Where was my Ivy League bravado, my lack of flexibility, my rigidity in purpose? They were all thrown out the window: desperation is the mother of adaptation and being open to change. If I was going to survive, it was time to transition from relying on academia and protocol to tapping into my intuitions and instincts. I could here the clock ticking. I was getting worse each day. I could not rule out anything.

Did you know that the offices of naturopaths not only feel different but smell different? Way different than the antiseptic aroma that permeates "normal" doctors' offices. Weird. But I could not have cared less at the time. I was dying. I needed someone to save my sorry ass.

His name was John.

John convinced me that Lyme disease was the culprit. He connected the dots. Things started to make sense. "Symptoms from different body systems can emanate from a single etiology," he explained. Then he sent me to a doctor who knew a great deal about Lyme disease. Unfortunately, John the naturopath died in his 40's. I am alive because of him. As I write this, I am almost sixty now. The irony of this has never left me. I regret never really thanking him. Thank you, John.

I spent thousands of lonely hours searching the Internet for information about Lyme and other tick-borne diseases. A whole new frontier. This was my introduction to a whole new area of controversy. While enormous evidence exists to prove persistent and chronic forms of these illnesses, an incensed debate rages within the medical community. Like it was not bad enough to suffer from these Lyme spirochetes drilling into every inch of my body, I now had to face the isolation and ridicule of so many who chose to believe the infectious disease physicians who denied the realities. Since I was well trained in doing my own research from earlier times in my life, I made sound judgments on the facts as I not only saw them but FELT them. It was like becoming a part of a group that was declaring the world round while the rest of society was insisting it was flat. The insulting and demeaning and belittling encounters were endless - not only with other lay people, but when it was necessary to see a physician. It was easy to get sucked into this war, but getting through the day provided me with enough battlefields and I made every effort to stay on task and pursue my own healing.

Still, it was upsetting and often felt defeating when people would roll their eyes when I mentioned "Lyme" or whispered behind my back or laughed outright to my face. My natural tendency is to shine a light on truth and talk to people about things that matter, but my husband and children were always warning me: "Don't mention Lyme to this person or that." They could not stand the tension that would ensue. Can you imagine? This was like throwing gasoline and a lit match on my anxiety.

Other diseases provoke feelings of compassion and kindness and handholding and homemade dinners delivered. I had the double misfortune to get an illness that provoked people to think I was a lunatic. There were no homemade dinners delivered. My husband picked up cooked chickens on his way home.

I was off to see Doctor S who taught me invaluable information about Lyme disease. Do you know what the most important thing he taught me was?

"LYME SUCKS."

This is what he wisely said over and over to me, visit after visit. I now believe there are no truer, no simpler words that were ever spoken. His validation of the inferno that was consuming me was a relief – sort of. Doctor S also taught me that Lyme is, in fact, a brain infection and very difficult to treat once it is becomes advanced. My case had progressed to a very advanced stage, no thanks to the hotshot, A-list doctors that have no clue what they are seeing.

Dr. S never said he could cure me. He tried to get the infection under control with various antibiotic combinations that provided a bit of relief. I could never have guessed that relief can only come after a hell storm called a Herxheimer reaction. It is a healing crisis. It was discovered years ago in Europe when penicillin was given to Syphilis patients and their symptoms got worse before they improved. Herxheimer reactions are caused by spirochete die off. This was a new dimension of misery for me to go through.

In the Lyme world these temporary episodes are called "herxes." Sometimes it's hard to distinguish between a herx and just being symptomatic. Some Lyme patients do not even care – they are so needy to celebrate something that every time they feel miserable they toast to their herx. So to all those people who swear they are better after their physicians pump gallons of meds into them for year after year, I say, "snap out of it!" I have spoken to dozens of people, all claiming to be much healthier after taking this medicine or that drug, only to hear them admit after they are done with their drug regimen that they are sicker than ever. It is true that I got some degree of functionality back while on meds but I still felt lousy. It was like I got a life back, but it was not my life. I was trapped in a body that felt like a loaded cannon. Every morning I took inventory of what body part or brain function would work or flare for that day. Within several months, I went from being bedridden to being able to walk a mile a day and I could once again resume minor errands. Still, life was marginalized, fragile, altered.

I will be forever grateful to Dr. S, however, for never giving me false hope or making hollow promises. His honesty was brutal. I used to tell him that he was a "doggie downer." He understood the enemy; it was formidable and he never tried to diminish it. Many hours were spent sobbing in his office parking lot after an appointment. I comprehended his language of realism and learned how to translate what he was NOT saying. I met many of his patients in his waiting room with stories like mine. Some worse. People with a myriad of misdiagnoses or Lyme-induced MS, Parkinson's, ALS, cardiac issues, Crohn's disease, celiac disease, and lupus to name just a few. He and other Lyme specialists got some people out of wheelchairs and saved some from heart transplants. One woman was almost blind and used a walker. After Lyme disease treatment, she was able to take a walking tour in Europe. I saw some amazing shifts towards functionality. But no cures. Most were still really sick. But I saw positive changes in people that were undeniable and inspiring.

After a total of sixty weeks of medication pulsed during a three plus year period, I started feeling a pull back into the alternative arena for better solutions. I was not interested in managing a long term, persistent disease; I wanted to reclaim full health – not just functionality.

Did I mention how expensive it is to have Lyme? I required a whole support team to make it through the week. Massages, colonics, acupuncture, and chiropractic care, to name only a few. Lyme costs a fortune. I could have fed an entire third world country with my never-to-be-reimbursed medical costs.

I logged a few really bad years living this way. I started eating really healthy. I gave up cigarettes, caffeine, alcohol and junk food. Tick-borne illnesses allow for no fun at all. There were no nights out, no easy travel. Getting through the day was a major accomplishment. Every day felt like walking on eggshells; I utterly compromised my lifestyle to avoid triggering any flare-ups. No decadence. No spontaneity. No fun.

I even had to forsake my love of nature and the outdoors. I was terrified of walking on the grass and being re-infected from a tick bite. I could not handle another exposure. The deer grazing in my front lawn all of a sudden seemed menacing. Simple joys like taking a walk on the grass were eliminated. Fear of re-infection governed my life and choices.

My older son called each morning from college with such concern in his voice that it broke my heart. He always wanted to know if I made it through the night alright and if anything was getting better. I was never any good at faking happiness or joy. My voice and constant crying always communicated more than he wanted to know.

My younger son was stuck with me. Poor kid. While my older son had grown up with a vivacious, fun, and engaging mom, my younger son spent years watching me suffer. I still get a lump in my throat when I think of how hard he tried to make me smile. Whether sitting on my bed and playing his guitar for me or just being his cheerful loving self - always "Hey Mama, you're getting better!" - trying to encourage me in every way. Always reaching for my hand to offer comfort. Without a doubt, I have the two kindest, most compassionate and loving sons that any woman could dream of having. I needed to move my mission forward. I owed it to them and did not want them to remember me as a sick person. I had expended oodles of love and fun on them so they would never have horrid childhood memories like the ones that still haunt my dreams. Just goes to show you that there are no limits to the number of ways to ruin a child's life.

My researching of options and alternatives began in earnest. At this point, I had spent several hours each day for more than three years trying to learn anything and everything about my condition. This was an extremely complicated arena. If tick-borne illnesses were, indeed, the etiology behind many other diagnoses, or if they – like syphilis – were profoundly imitating these illnesses, the ramifications were tremendous. While ticks have been around for thousands of years, there seemed to be a significant shift in the type of damage they could cause. There are many theories on the why and how this is: I had read the book *LAB 257* about Plum Island and Operation Paper Clip that ensued post World War II. Intriguing. Since the Plum Island lab was in the Long Island Sound, and ground zero for Lyme disease was just across the water along the Connecticut coastline, it was hard to dismiss such pieces of information. Did experiments on ticks go amiss? Maybe. Some claimed that the overabundance of the deer population was spreading this disease like wildfire. Others surmised that more people had moved out of cities to areas with greater risk for exposure. There were a lot of pieces that did not add up. I began to see things though an entirely different filter.

When I was growing up, I had never heard of so many conditions and diseases that were now plaguing our society. Autism? ADHD? Fibromyalgia? Chronic fatigue? Who ever heard of these things? A third of my son's class by first grade was medicated with Ritalin or Adderall or other drugs. Back then, I thought it was because of bad parenting and no limits. Now I could not help wondering if these children had been unknowingly infected while playing outside. And why did so many children all of a sudden have a myriad of food allergies when my generation could eat TV dinners and Twinkies and devil dogs and Wonder Bread and complete garbage with no issues? And why did so many children have such horrid emotional issues? Other generations had survived wars, depressions, and other assorted miseries. Everyone seemed more fragile now. Almost every adult was being medicated for anxiety or depression. Pills were being dispensed everywhere. When had sick become normal? People were starting to blame vaccinations. My instincts did not buy that argument. I would hate to go back to the days where diseases like polio could strike the public.

I had many friends that were getting cancers, Parkinson's, and MS all before they were 40-years old. In fact, I did not know a single household where at least one person did not have a serious ailment. And like I said, the drugs were flowing everywhere. It really started to seem like our system was designed to keep people medicated and sick instead of attempting to unravel the etiologies and provide resolution. More drugs. The phrase "follow the money" would ring in my ever-sensitive ears over and over.

I started reaching out to my friends who had these horrible diagnoses. "Did you ever get tested for Lyme disease or Mycoplasma or Babesia? Maybe your husband's MS is Lyme. Maybe your Parkinson's is tick-borne." It amazed me how many people would hold fast to their death sentence instead of pushing the boundaries of the establishment to seek more answers. Another Lyme patient always said to me of these people: "They just LOVE their diagnoses of MS or ALS. They are attached."

I was baffled. I knew several people who had been given horrid MS verdicts with bleak prospects who had responded to Lyme treatment. One woman who had been in a wheelchair with her "MS" was later treated for Lyme and recovered enough to walk, ride a bike, drive, and resume working. Sure, she still had issues – like back surgery and shoulder surgery – but she never went back to her hell zone. And yet, most people I talked to just backed away and viewed me as insane when I tried to share anecdotal stories.

I kept noticing how filled with rage people were. Who knew road rage was so rampant? Who thirty years ago had heard of so many random shootings? Or high numbers of teen suicides? No one can eat gluten anymore? Seriously? Who knew what the hell gluten was thirty years ago? And so many young people – children, teenagers, young professionals – marginalized in a myriad of ways. A slice of pizza or a bite of a cookie should not be setting off volcanic reactions in people's bodies. Not to mention the staggering rise of lifelong debilitating diseases diagnosed in children: diabetes, childhood cancers, autism...the list goes on of what is keeping children's hospitals across the country overwhelmed.

Young and middle-aged people were getting more and more body parts replaced. Hips, knees...it reminded me of my old Mr. Potato Head game: pull a part out and stick it back in again. It became difficult to ignore the growing number of wheelchairs and scooters and walkers and canes that were being used by people not even close to approaching geriatric age. Navigating public spaces was like cautiously walking though a bumper car game at the amusement park. How did everyone become so disabled? Strolling the boardwalk at the Jersey Shore could be downright depressing. There were more people on scooters than should have ever been imaginable. The contrast was startling on vacations to other places where everyone – even the 80-year old men – was full of vitality, walking, running, rollerblading, and seemingly whole. I am sure I would have ended up with a scooter or worse had I not finally gotten an accurate diagnosis.

Yes, I was not imagining all this. Diseases in America were on the rise in a huge way. If you remember where you were when President John F. Kennedy was shot, you probably remember a society of healthy people. If you are younger...well...all I can say is if they gave punch cards at pharmacies like they do in coffee shops and restaurants, there would be a whole lot of free drugs being dispensed.

So how many people are carrying a bacterial infection from tick exposure that might be an underlying cause of some issues? I have NO IDEA. But guess what? The physicians have NO IDEA either because no one is checking for it. And no one is seeking etiology and resolution. They just keep drugging and suppressing the symptoms.

Again, I felt pulled into the alternative arena for answers and solutions.

We had a broken steam room in our house. I started to think that I should repair it to sweat out some of the drug toxins and maybe take a load off my immune system. The repair quote was $1500. No way. I was already planning my exit strategy to leave the tick infested woods of Connecticut as soon as my youngest child graduated high school. Adios. I was certainly not putting that money into a non-portable device. After poking around the Internet for some other options, I discovered the world of infrared sauna therapy. Over the next few months, I read books and articles galore about sauna therapy and the myriad of benefits. This not only became my next purchase, it became the fulcrum upon which my entire view about health, medicine, and healing would shift.

Ah, the infrared sauna. What started out as a simple plan to detox the antibiotics and medications that served as my body's marinade for three years ended up being a game changer. Case in point: I had spent my whole life administering Advil and Tylenol to my family whenever fever would strike. Even a low-grade fever. Now I was purchasing a modality to create an artificial fever to rev up the immune system and have the body combat pathogens and illness with its own defenses. I never realized that a fever was nature's own reliable way to have the body defeat invaders. I felt like a moron. I needed to learn more about working in partnership with my body's own arsenal of healing tools. I did not want to spend the rest of my life on antibiotics to keep from going under.

You want to get over taking pills to feel better? Get a tick-borne illness. There are not enough pills out there to keep you functional. We Americans are trained to take pills to feel better. I have encountered people who are taking up to 26 different pharmaceuticals a day. Pills to sleep, pills to wake up, pills for anxiety, pills for depression, pills for pain – to mention a few. Pills that fill television ad spots with images of happy people enjoying life. Pills that make people dependent on pharmaceuticals forever because they only veil the problems – the hurt, the pain, the suffering – rather than offering a permanent cure. And don't forget about those fun side effects and warnings!

When the infrared sauna got delivered, I commenced my journey out of illness toward health. It would be a long journey with a mosaic of modalities, but the infrared sauna was the first awakening that my body had intuitive powers to heal itself. When I first sat inside this nice, warm, soothing contraption, I could have never imagined what was happening inside my body.

Infrared saunas do not get hot like steam rooms or regular saunas. They feel more like sitting at the pool in Las Vegas in July. They work with something called resonant absorption and frequency stuff. It felt so good inside the sauna - nothing hurt at all. I was loving the moment. No pain. But during the hours and days following the initial treatments, the healing reactions were intense. The stuff that was coming out of my body was disgusting. Mucus, phlegm, sinus congestion, bladder pain, and a myriad of skin eruptions where toxins were trying to escape.

I had never thought of my skin being the largest organ of my body until that point. I have never put any lotions and creams on my skin that were not 100% chemical-free since getting my sauna. They say if you cannot eat it, do not put it on your skin. I left the world of high cosmetics and fancy perfumed creams for organic coconut oils, shea butters, and other natural and healthy skin treatments. It did not take long for me to convert everyone else in the family, too.

Some of my healing reactions to the sauna therapy were positively otherworldly. The message was clear: my body was loaded with all sorts of bad things. Bugs. Metals. Residual traces of past infections and G-d knows what else. I could not fool myself any longer. The medications had given me functionality by suppressing the symptoms and disease, but they never eradicated much. The sauna treatments showed me how deeply embedded my illness was. The first months of sauna therapy were uncomfortable at best. They even included one trip to the emergency room. This infrared sauna – this nice, warm, soothing contraption – was a weapon.

Over the years, I have seen some crazy sauna healing reactions. I had a neighbor who complained of arthritis, fibromyalgia, depression, fibro-fog (when she used to drive around lost or hit dividers in the road). All sorts of misery. She had her own list of hotshot, A-listers. I told her I thought she had Lyme disease. She thought I was insane. She came over to try my sauna one day and felt oh so good inside. No pain and went home a happy camper. I told her she would get a healing reaction that might cause her to feel quite sick. She went home and threw up and had diarrhea for hours.

Lost five pounds. No joke. She then went for a Lyme test and was positive on even the inadequate Quest test.

What did her A-lister tell her? False positive!

A symptomatic woman with a positive test. Can you imagine that? Isn't that beyond unbelievable?

I was now at a real crossroads. I had to make a decision to move forward in this arena of resolving things instead of suppressing things. Sure, I wanted to feel better but now it was more important to BE better and strive for health. Even if it meant enduring a long and arduous process. The differences between allopathic physicians and naturopathic and holistic practitioners started to become pronounced. And while I commend the allopathic medical world for what they do in trauma centers and operating rooms and so many other arenas, when it comes to chronic infections and general well-being, there are serious shortcomings. Very serious ones.

Holistic healing provides no quick fixes. It demands the patient go through many healing reactions and retracing patterns of past conditions and ailments that have built up in the body and marginalized the immune system. Was I up for this challenge?

There are seemingly ordinary days that can end up changing your life in profound ways. You just need to be aware of the signals and opportunities that arrive under the umbrella of destiny. And so it was, the day and moment that would impact my life and the lives of hundreds of others that would cross my path from that day forward.

It started as a simple outing to a local book store. My husband and son headed for the music section. I normally immerse myself in the fiction and literature area, but this time I ended up in the medical section – a place I never approached because I got so creeped out by illness and disease. Also, I thought of reading as a pleasurable escape from life and did not want to be mired in volumes of science and medicine. But as I brushed by a bookshelf, a book caught my attention – one I have never seen in a bookstore since and the hundreds of people who purchased it after me have only been able to buy it online. Destiny? Fate? A gift from a higher power?

The book that saved my life: *WHEN ANTIBIOTICS FAIL. LYME DISEASE AND RIFE MACHINES* by Bryan Rosner. I was almost too nervous to touch it. I knew after years of antibiotics that I was still sick - but did I want to read and validate the "fail" part?

So I went from the bookshelf to the floor and eventually to a chair to immerse myself in this book. My mind and my body were telling me that this book spoke of truth. And while I was no scientist or physician, I was quite the expert on my own body and I knew I was still a very sick puppy, that the disease inside of me had set up base camp in my brain – a very difficult place for antibiotics to reach – and that the enemy spirochetes were positively ferocious in their determination to evade and survive any onslaught or attack. Rosner explained how spirochetes hiding in cyst form can be the undoing of the patient: the human host. Just when you think there are periods of progress, you are eventually proven wrong when the infectious agents come out of cyst form to wreak more havoc on your suffering body.

Rosner had my attention. I knew a tiny bit about Royal Rife, an inventor who in the early 1900s had made a super powerful microscope and experimented with applying frequencies to pathogens to facilitate their demise. He worked with mortal oscillatory rates (MOR's) to determine which frequencies could destroy which pathogens. The common analogy used is to that of an opera singer shattering a glass when a specific note or frequency is struck. Apparently, Rosner and many others had experienced a decent level of recovery from their respective ailments (a number of them from Lyme disease) by experimenting with different frequency machines in their wars against bugs.

I expanded my research during the ensuing months. I read volumes of information and watched a multitude of videos that illustrated how frequencies could dismantle certain bugs in a matter of seconds. I wanted to find a frequency machine to use on myself. Not so easy to do. I could not find anyone who owned one. There were certain practitioners, operating below the radar, who were charging money for patients to use their machines. But I figured that it was smarter for me to invest in my own machine. Not FDA approved, a frequency machine is one of those things that you experiment with at your own risk. My husband thought I was crazy. My friends warned me that I would hurt myself. But in my quiet desperation to feel whole again, I was willing to take new chances. Remember, I had learned the hard way that my survival was not a top priority for the mainstream medical community. I was on my own. Scary.

During my months of research – while the bugs inside of me were munching and multiplying – I found a woman in the next town who was also curious about this unconventional modality. We decided to split the cost of a machine and do our own experimenting. And so my journey into the underground began.

With a total stranger and a totally strange machine. Insane. Did I mention how desperate I was?

We purchased a GB4000 frequency generator with an amplifier. A pretty blue-purplish box with a few wires and some handles. We called ourselves the "cliff jumpers" since we felt like Butch Cassidy and the Sundance Kid jumping off the cliff into the unknown. In the meantime, my husband, after initially giving me a hard time about purchasing the GB4000 – who turned out to also be infected with Lyme disease – decided he wanted in on the action and jumped off the cliff with us. Curious and recognizing that I had done my homework, he saw this leap of faith as an experiment. And if he could restore some of his own health as well, even better. So off we went, the three of us, into a whole new realm. We have never looked back.

So the three of us cliff jumpers started to experiment with different frequencies and auto channels. Herxheimer reactions were immediate. Some reactions were familiar, like headaches, fatigue, anxiety, and muscle pain. Other reactions were new and varied, like itchy skin and intense sugar cravings. It seemed like each time we played with new frequencies or turned the dial up that our reactions were predictably unpredictable. Every time I went on the machine, I always had exploding floaters in my left eye and considerable dry eye that was worse than ever before. I had read that when you start experimenting with frequencies, that you find there are bugs everywhere in your body that have been hiding out. Although knee pain was a common tick-borne symptom, I had never experienced it until I started firing frequencies into my body. Bam! Ugh! Knee pain walking up the stairs. I would have predictable crying jags within 48 hours: sore throat, ear pain, mouth sores, and many more reactions to this experimental modality. WOW!

We cliff jumpers spent a lot of time laughing through our misery, wondering how we could learn about what we were experiencing. Talk about trial and error. But somehow we moved our mission forward. People who had ridiculed us for branching out in this direction were now showing up at our houses to sneak a peek at the machine or to ask us questions. Everyone was nervous to branch out, but people were more nervous about not healing through traditional means.

More and more people started getting machines. Our network was mushrooming along the East Coast. It was not long until there were hundreds of us, all experimenting in our own individual ways with how to apply frequencies into our bodies to try to annihilate microbes that were hurting us. People started swapping information and digging into their own research. We were a resourceful group. And while the first year was not so easy, we somehow seemed able to do more activities and reclaim some vitality.

Terms like "harmonics" and "sweeping" and "channel sweeping" – paired with all sorts of numbers – were part of the learning curve. Researching what others had done, even in far reaching countries around the world, added to our anecdotal database. It was like learning a whole new language – and I was never good at foreign languages. Still, it seemed proactive and empowering to have something in the privacy of our own homes that we could experiment with on our own terms, at our own rate, and allow our bodies to become the doctors, in a sense, by dictating how much we could do or not do. I got comfortable with this machine fairly quickly. It became my best friend. I figured, as long as I had electricity, I could keep myself alive. It was like playing Space Invaders in my body: I envisioned blowing the little bugs apart, slowly but surely, putting out the awful fire of hell inside me. It reminded me of words that Flannery O'Connor once wrote: "If you don't hunt it down and kill it, it will hunt you down and kill you."

We fell into a rhythm of continual experimentation and efforts to clear the debris from our bodies. Kill, clear, kill. Many of us used various types of saunas to help detox the garbage while others used enormous amounts of Epsom salt baths. Various other tricks and tools were tried by all: lemon water, parsley, ionic foot baths, and colonics among them. Detoxing was a constant challenge.

There was a naturopath, let's call him Dr. A, who was very savvy with frequency modalities. He had an EAV machine, which is used largely in Europe. EAVs are electro-acupuncture devices, developed by a German medical doctor and engineer. Most allopathic people in the United States would consider this machine ridiculous. Not FDA-approved – but few things are approved that do not direct people and their funds toward drugs and more drugs. I found the EAV interesting and looked at its energetic and meridian components as additional information for where my body was most stressed out from the infection. The EAV also helped determine which frequencies to utilize to target the bugs. There were so many things out there in the holistic and alternative world to try. Some were more interesting than others. I liked the EAV.

While dealing with Dr. A, I learned that I had acute metal toxicity and mercury poisoning. I had read papers by many physicians about mercury poisoning and Lyme disease – how the mercury can suppress the immune system and the Lyme bugs attach to it and create quite a big mess in the body. I had amalgam fillings in my mouth since I was 3 years old. And when I started with Dr. A, I had 8 fillings in my adult teeth. No surprise that I was loaded with metal toxicity.

I could write a whole book on this topic – and several people have already – but all I can say is that you have to question having a substance implanted in your body right near your brain that is illegal to be thrown in the trash can. Yes. You read that correctly. At least in the state of Connecticut, amalgam fillings must be discarded as hazardous waste. But America is still a country where it is legal to put mercury in the human body. Talk about insanity. Follow the money...need I say more?

I could not make this insanity up. And yet the masses follow like sheep, believing whatever they are told without questioning. I am ashamed to say I was one of those people who trusted the authorities. But when you get so intensely and incredibly sick and no one has answers, then questioning becomes essential to survival.

So off to the holistic dentist I went, and out came those eight amalgams that were leeching mercury into my body 24/7. Using chelators and binders to try to mop up the mess inside me was a whole other nightmare. Chelating metals is not fun. Another misery.

The chelation experience landed me back in the emergency room. I fell apart completely when the mercury was mobilized in my brain. Wow. There are no words for my suffering. It felt like the Lyme spirochetes were let loose and charging my body with a vengeance that was unrelenting. I had to halt the mobilizing and calm things back down in my body. So binders like chlorella were all my body could handle to try to mop up the metals. I must have consumed truckloads of chlorella in the past five years; it will likely continue being part of my daily routine forever.

I used Dr. A for a myriad of things, including biofeedback treatments to get my anxiety under control. The anxiety had me spiraling into a galaxy of perpetual hell. He did neurotransmitter testing by sending body fluids to some lab, which confirmed that my whole body was completely fried. He tried to balance me with supplements. And I did ionic foot baths and a few other things at his office. Then I moved away and had to search for a practitioner who was more accessible. But during my period of desperation, Dr. A was amazingly kind and supportive and there for me in countless ways. He navigated me through all sorts of hysteria and fear with compassion that other physicians seemed to lack. So grateful for him.

Like a steady drumbeat, my frequency machine and I made beautiful music together. Bam! Pow! Yikes! I would try anything. Parasites, mold, fungus, worms. Eye disorders, ear disorders, nerve disorders. There was no end to the options for experimentation. Always new frequencies and new techniques. Longer run times. Longer sweep times. More and more and more.

While frequencies and the infrared sauna were the staples of my journey at this point, there was always a new "out there" modality to try to repair my broken body. It was like my body was a house on fire, but even though the frequencies were able to put out the flames, my body was destroyed and needed more than the fire department. I needed a carpenter, plumber, electrician, painter, and a whole host of other people to try to put my torched body back together – kind of like Humpty Dumpty. Now, my team was better than all the king's horses and king's men. I had some awesome holistic practitioners and physicians that used some very cool healing tools. And they all had one thing in common: the belief that the body has the ability and desire to heal itself, as long as you can remove interference so it has a fighting chance.

It has become commonplace for people with assorted ailments, and even healthy people, to read about nutritional supplements online, then stroll through supermarket aisles and health food stores to amass a collection of vitamins and herbs to ingest each day. I was one of those people, and Lyme people in general take a ridiculous amount of supplements. The more I thought about it, however the more I started to feel nervous. For one, I had no idea what was really in all these things. And secondly, I really had no idea how all these things would interact with each other in my body. It was like being a chemistry experiment, even though the stuff was not by prescription. My body was already working so damn hard at this point that I started wondering if "less was more." I did not want to keep pumping products into my body just because the latest blog, article, or expert declared "YOU NEED THIS!"

Applied kinesiology and muscle testing used to seem foolish and ridiculous to me, but once again, it was time to reflect and reevaluate my rigidity. I decided that muscle testing was better than random selection. It might not be foolproof, but it was better than shoving ten million supplements down my throat each day. That is when I discovered Dr. D, who had a zillion certifications in nutrition and applied kinesiology and many modalities. Not only did he eliminate most of the supplements I was taking that were stressing out my body, but he fine-tuned my nutrition in a way that - at the very least - allowed me to not have to shop around and read all about various options; at the very best, I was actually starting to put into my body things that would facilitate my recovery.

Dr. D introduced me to many energetic modalities like TBM (total body modification), NET (neuro-emotional technique), B.E.S.T. (bio energetic synchronization techniques), and NMT (neuro modulation technique). I had previously met a woman who was excellent at TBM, and I had already used her technique to clear boatloads of emotional trauma to free up my body to heal. But Dr. D was the master of NMT and knew how to stabilize the body like no other. The NMT uses muscle response testing to address different pathways in the body – toxic, sensory, infectious, allergic, emotional, etc – to see what is the top priority of the moment.

Now I know muscle testing seems like bullshit to many people, but for me and many others I know, this was an essential option. When the priority is established, the doctor uses an arthrostim to tap and stimulate the spine while the patient breathes in and out, deeply and rhythmically. These treatments are repeated and repeated and repeated to continually, one by one, remove the top obstacles in the bodies healing process. We call them clearings. And they seem to dovetail nicely with the hits on the frequency machines, which tend to stir up a bit of commotion in infected people. Dr. D was enormously helpful, respectful, supportive and resourceful. A true stabilizer. He saved the day so many times for so many of us. We are eternally grateful. In fact, after working with him, the trips to the emergency room ceased.

At this point, I was always scouting out new therapies to further my mission in reclaiming my health. There were many alternative modalities I tried, and then dismissed as non-effective. Then one night, I attended a lecture given by an upper cervical specialist: Dr. G. She explained that when the top two vertebrae near the brainstem are misaligned, it creates chaos and interference between the brain and the rest of the central nervous system and body. These two important skeletal items are the atlas and axis. Since the brain is the mission control room that sends messaging to every part of the body, the ideal situation for optimal functioning and healing is to remove any subluxation that is obstructing information. It is a non-invasive and simple procedure that very few chiropractors specialize in.

This presentation resonated with me. The simplicity and logic of it all made this a literal "no brainer" to investigate. So off I went to have my C1 and C2 adjusted, or, in plain English, have my head put on straight. Apparently, the central nervous system is like a computer that stores data from every illness and injury the body has endured. So when the atlas and axis become aligned – for probably the first time in years and possibly since birth – it is like flicking the circuit breakers in your house and all the electricity comes on. Wow. Intense. Like you would not believe how intense this experience can be. It initiates a natural healing process as the body begins to operate properly, and you go through a process called "retracing" through which old injuries and symptoms are revisited. Over a period of months, I literally re-felt old ankle sprains and a myriad of other things, including an ancient recurring zit in the corner of my nose that I had not seen since high school. The body is really a brilliant machine.

The retracing only lasted a few months for me. After that, however, there were still roller coaster emotions, fatigue, and a surge of detoxification. It was like I was bouncing along in a jeep in the jungle, stopping to use a machete to cut down brush in the way and removing boulders before I could continue driving. Every time I cleared an obstacle in my path, my central nervous system was back at optimal functioning, and all of a sudden I would be just cruising along. Then a few weeks (and after time, a few months) later, I would need a readjustment. This proved to be a great and simple modality that is essential to facilitating brain and body communication. It helped me move forward and made me feel less vulnerable.

I started making concrete and measurable progress. I could participate in life like a semi-normal person again. I was walking between four to eight miles a day. I could recognize myself in photographs again. There were years when my face had taken on a very "neuro" look. It is hard to describe, but I looked fried. Which is how I felt, of course...but I really looked fried when I saw myself in the mirror. Many of my crazy medical anomalies were unwinding to a point that they would surface less frequently and, when they did, it was with less intensity and a shorter duration. My body was working so hard to repair itself. I was awed by its valiant efforts.

As time went on, I was experimenting aggressively with different frequency runs. It was easier to handle the runs, and the Herxheimer reactions became minimal or non-existent. I went after everything like a savage at this point. My body was getting stronger – I could handle it. I had amazing support therapies in place and a wonderful massage therapist who helped coax my body through the journey back to health. He is the closest thing to a healing saint that I have ever known. His gifted hands are remarkable, but his generosity of spirit and intuitive sense of what is happening in the body is truly unique.

I had been to many physicians – including neurologists – and holistic practitioners and, of course, emergency room doctors about the recurring feeling that my head felt split into two disjointed parts. Right down the middle. I complained to everyone about it and no one seemed to grasp what I was saying. Nothing showed up on a brain MRI and everyone kind of rolled their eyes at me. Yet, my massage therapist felt it with his hands and I never even told him about it. Go figure. I cried and whined to every medical doctor in the universe and they shrugged - like "WTF" are you talking about - while my massage therapist put his hands on my head and said: "Sista, you got something weird happening in there that I have never felt before." Bless him. And bless his hands.

By that point I had simply accepted that I had certain things that were permanent nerve damage from when the bugs shorted out my central nervous system. So I had stopped complaining about my head being split into two and started enjoying the many parts of my life and health that I was reclaiming. And then I met a physician who was nothing short of a magician. His name was Dr. J.

Dr. J was in his 30s. Casual. Cute. And usually had an entourage of medical students that hung on his every word. To say this guy was a bit "out of the box" is an understatement. In his own words: "When G-d made me, he took away everything but my hands." I have no clue what was taken away, but those hands have been working miracles on me and many others I know. But when I first met him, I had no idea what his abilities were. So imagine my shock when he put his hands on my head to administer cranial osteopathy and then I heard him telling the medical students in the room: "This patient has no integration between the left and right side of her brain." I jumped off the table and practically cried! I was so taken aback completely that his hands felt what no other physician could even understand, and I had not even mentioned it to him. When I inquired whether or not it was repairable, he said yes. I almost fainted from shock. It was years and many doctors later from my first emergency room visit for this issue, and here was someone who nonchalantly said he could fix it. Can you believe?

I was wholly unfamiliar with cranial osteopathy work. And I could not have believed in a million years what could ensue after a treatment. Supposedly, a skilled cranial practitioner can feel and adjust the potency of one's central nervous system by gently manipulating the skeleton and connective tissues. It feels gentle and relaxing. In fact, one can barely feel anything during a session. So after my first treatment, which seemed like a non-event, I went home and was slammed with the most acute and unrelenting fatigue I have ever experienced. Over a period of several days, I had flashing red lights in my left eye, head pain on the left side that felt like I was black and blue in my brain, hair loss, crying jags, and overall misery. To say I was freaked out was an understatement. I said to my husband: "Could this guy be hurting me?" It was difficult to imagine that these reactions could occur after feeling like the guy barely touched me, but it felt like I had come out of brain surgery without the knives.

After a series of these treatments and reactions, I can honestly say that my brain felt integrated and whole again. It was astonishing. In fact, my massage therapist felt the change with his own hands and said he never felt anything like it. Like Moses parting the Red Sea. It felt miraculous to me. I never thought my head would feel normal again.

In fact, when the flow of the cerebrospinal fluid was stimulated over time, it felt like a toilet plunger had gone into my brain and sucked out all the neurotoxins from the disease. It was like pooping and peeing and sweating could help move the toxins out of my body, but the ones in my brain were stuck - very stuck until this modality helped release them. Dr. J understood how formidable the Lyme infection was. I continually heard him tell medical students that Lyme was a "traumatic brain injury" and that once it hits the brain stem, it is "lights out." Yes - he had amazing comprehension of the topic and learned much of it from working on people's heads and bodies that were infected.

How could it be that some of these alternative modalities that I never heard of or would have considered ten years prior - things I would have dismissed and ridiculed - ended up contributing so much to reversing my downward spiral and allowing my body to recover from utter devastation?

Ancient essential oils, Chinese medicine, Ayurvedic medicine, meditation, and shamanic guidance are only a few of the healing systems that could enlighten us. The way a young adult dismisses the wisdom of the elderly, we modern Americans seem to have 'thrown the baby out with the bathwater.' So much of our medical system is based on new and innovative pharmaceuticals that we have lost respect for the medical wisdom of those who came before the last hundred years. Maybe if we are lucky we can somehow integrate the medicine and knowledge of the patriarchs and matriarchs of medicine with the modern research and development that provides us with life saving procedures and medications. I imagine that many of our new wonder drugs will fall away into the abyss of horrid side effects, while the frankincense and myrrh from biblical times will still have a niche in the worldwide medical arena.

I would never pretend to have all the answers for everyone. Dealing with Lyme disease is a humbling experience. It taught me to embrace change and opportunity - to be less rigid and to become resourceful. It would be tempting to say that several treatments and practitioners were a waste of time, but these experiences taught me what did NOT work and forced me to be judicious with my assessments of what had a positive impact.

Winston Churchill said, "If you're going through hell, keep going," and that is exactly what I did. Finding the exit door out of the Lyme inferno was my primary objective. My family needed me whole again - or at least not completely broken and helpless. I have tried to create new and happy memories with them so they do not remember me as sick and needy. I have tried to bring love and joy into their lives and to be present for them, and I believe they know how hard I worked for them to not be abandoned. We take walks, eat out, enjoy vacations and holidays and simple pleasures that feel miraculous to me now. I sob at each milestone I observe with awe as I never thought I would survive. They know I will cry. They do not try to stop me. They know I am not sad but overwhelmed with gratitude and love.

Every time I visited my older son at college, we visited the spot where I lost feeling in my legs. I wept every time I made that pilgrimage, including on the day he graduated. I would have never believed four years earlier that I would live to see that day.

I would say that no one could ever heal from anything without some unconditional love and kindness from those closest to them. It is the one unwavering truth and reality. The rest of the modalities - they can be visited and tried and experimented – but the love is essential.

Sometimes I feel like there are two groups of people on the East Coast of the United States: those who are infected and know it, and those who are infected and think they have something else. There was a quote from a favorite Pat Conroy novel that was posted on our refrigerator for years:

"My friends had always come from outside the mainstream. I had always been popular with the fifth column of my peers, those individuals who were princely in their solitude, lords of their own unpraised melancholy. Distrusting the approval of the chosen, I would take the applause of exiles anytime. My friends were all foreigners, and they wore their unbelongingness in their eyes. I hunted for that look; I saw it often, disarrayed and fragmentary and furious..."

While the Lyme disease journey is a lonely and isolating one, it is like being in a war where you truly find other warriors like yourself. I remember a friend whose husband fought in Vietnam and she said twenty years later if they were anywhere, at any function, and there was one other Vietnam veteran in attendance, they would inevitably find each other - even if it was in a crowd of 200 people. I understand those words now better than when I heard them. The people in the Lyme war that fought with everything and left the comfort and "safeness" of respectability to be ridiculed and mocked in pursuit of the correct diagnosis and the alternative modalities and remedies are people who were and are my fellow foreigners and warriors.

There are many I have encountered - hundreds from many states. Their stories are all the same in some ways, yet each as unique as a fingerprint. It is the nature of the illness.

Like James, who made a promise to his newborn daughter that he would overcome his initial diagnosis of multiple sclerosis so that she would know him.

Like Alexandra, whose son Mike was one of the countless children taking ADHD medication; he took it for ten years and she fought like a lioness after she got a delayed correct Lyme diagnosis, which ended up being the underlying etiology for her son's misery.

Like with Ann, who had so many symptoms and such unimaginable pain that the allopathic physicians ultimately had her living each day on 26 different pharmaceuticals.

And then there are people like Jason, who did not personally suffer from Lyme disease, but offers another perspective as someone who witnessed its toll on his family and the families of countless others.

The stories are endless. These are just a few.

Lyme disease does not discriminate. It is a great equalizer. I have seen people with billions of dollars brought to their knees. Royalty. Celebrities. Major hedge fund owners. People whose families donated wings to major hospitals. Poor people. Adults. Children. Every race and religion. It does not matter who you are or how much money you have. You are screwed. And no one is going to take care of you – at least more than yourself. The sooner you accept that it is ultimately up to you to save yourself, the sooner you will take steps to reclaiming your life.

I do not know how many years this disease has taken off my

life expectancy, or what off-shoot of this will hunt me down and kill me. It is hard to imagine that someone's immune system can be so compromised for so many years that they will not be taken down eventually.

Did I triumph completely? Did I postpone or slow down the inevitable? I have no idea. But I tried my best to adhere to medicine's finest and only true top-notch, hotshot, A-lister's advice:

"IF YOU ARE NOT YOUR OWN DOCTOR, YOU ARE A FOOL."
Hippocrates, C. 460-400 BC

CALL ME JAMES

I am the father that refuses to die. My beautiful daughter was born in 2006. At first touch, she tightly grabbed my finger and would not let go. I have always held that feeling, that knowledge of her new life and the instant love inside my heart, mind, and soul. Within a few months of her birth, I was diagnosed with Multiple Sclerosis. I was 36 years old. I had a horrible prognosis, but my new baby daughter became my focus, my mission to live – to win over disease and death. I promised her that year that she would know her father.

It started with impaired memory and concentration. Numbness ascended my body from my toes. I had vision imbalance, difficulty swallowing, loss of taste, incredible fatigue, and extreme headaches. I had to sleep between work appointments. Visits to the emergency room provided no help. A leading doctor had checked me over. Our talk ended on the numbness in my legs. He apparently had gotten ascending numbness in his legs once when playing tennis, so he told me it would just go away within a couple of days. He was wrong.

My wife and I started searching for neurologists and

trudging around to all of them. After seeing a prominent one in New England, I had MRI work done which indicated I had over 23 lesions on my brain and spinal cord! Not to mention a herniated disc C5/C6. Within a week of this test, I was non-functional and bedridden. I would stay this way for a year.

I cried rivers. My wife would come home from work only to see me bawling in pain while drowning in the fear and sadness of the unknown. I would go to bed unable to sleep. I remember screaming into a pillow to be quiet while pulling my hair, holding my head and crying. Wondering if I was contagious, I feared touching my wife or daughter. The first two neurologists gave me a firm MS diagnosis with a horrible prognosis. They offered up chemotherapy and a wheelchair. They were simply writing me off.

A colleague of my wife suggested I have a test for Lyme disease, since it often presents as MS or can cause MS. I believe in the MS arena, there is just MS, there is Lyme-induced MS, and there is Lyme disease that mimics or acts and looks like MS. In fact, if you look at maps of MS and Lyme disease cases in the United States, they match up almost identically. It makes you wonder.

We asked the neurologist to put me on antibiotics, as he could not guarantee this was not caused by a Lyme infection. We lived in a rural part of New England and I had ample opportunities for tick exposure in the great and beautiful outdoors. I had grown up in the Midwest and remember pulling ticks off me, not knowing of the potential diseases they carried. The doctor put me on minocycline and

I actually started to feel a bit better. But he said it only acted as an anti-inflammatory. In the meantime, I was on betaseron interferon for a month. I tried to have him work with me to see the effects of antibiotics, which were the standard Lyme disease treatments, versus other medications for the MS. I ended the relationship with him except for follow-up MRIs because I felt the antibiotics were helping and the MS interferon injections were only making me worse.

Furthermore, he put me on steroids and it ruined me. I had 10,000 grams infused. The withdrawal itself was murder. I haggled with life daily. We also discovered during this time that steroids actually feed bacteria since they suppress the immune system and create an unchallenged environment for bugs to multiply. I will never take steroids again. Ever. They made me far worse and elevated all my symptoms.

My wife found a website on Chlamydia Pneumonia, or CPN, as she was still out on maternity leave. This site was a haven for MS patients who were treating their MS with antibiotics and supplements and getting better. CPN is a respiratory infection that apparently everyone has, but every person's body handles it differently. Supposedly. We found research that was done forty years prior in France with high doses of tetracycline and patients were doing well into their 90's. So we flew to Tennessee to see the leading CPN doctor. Simply walking through the airport was difficult. I resisted wheelchair use and pushed myself to move properly. After my appointment, I began the treatment of supplements. At this point, I was literally taking 25 pills, twice a day – in addition to neurologist antibiotics. After a follow-up MRI to examine changes in the brain, cervical and thoracic regions – two hours flat on the scan table, no movement that could mess up alignment – my brother drove me home. I couldn't climb the stairs without him directing me up to bed.

There was a third neurologist I saw at this point for further opinion. This one was a leading Lyme disease neurology specialist. He wanted me off antibiotics for two weeks to do a spinal tap and retest me for Lyme disease. Within one day of going off the minocycline, I fell apart completely. I never did the spinal tap since I jumped back on the antibiotics immediately knowing it had positive movement forward. This neurologist said I was "Too far gone."

It was time to start pushing the envelope and pulling out other treatment options to keep myself going. I remembered my promise I made to my baby daughter. I am a man of my word and my love for her and my wife made me determined to persevere. Without them? I do not know what I would have done.

I started Chlamydia Pneumonia treatment on my own. I even purchased antibiotics online as we researched, tested and needed. We then found a Lyme disease literate physician and an infectious disease doctor who were willing to treat me for Lyme and other tick-borne infections. At this point, blood work done through IGeneX, Inc. finally revealed three reactive bands positive for chronic Lyme disease, also with Babesiosis, Bartonella, Mycoplasma, Candida, CPN, and other viruses. In fact, I learned at this point that many people with Lyme disease also have CPN. These physicians treated me very aggressively for my bug infections and I started to regain functionality in life. I did Rocephin IV first, then Rocephin and Tigecycline IV together. I was no longer bedridden. I was starting to experience brief glimpses into normalcy or what felt like before Lyme disease took me down. They have been called "windows." There was an early "window" day that completely amazed my wife. I had energy, cleaned myself up, straightened the house and hung up many pictures – handling all chores we had discussed doing for a long time. When she came home from work, she was shocked at what I had accomplished!

My daughter was no longer a baby and I showered her with love each day. It was like I was trying to fuel her up with love, topping off her tank in case I ran out. It was a precarious time but I was pushing through. I had MRIs every few months to follow treatment and my lesions began to disappear. I only had 10 left! This was progress indeed.

I figured at this point that I would survive on antibiotics for the rest of my life. A little bit of a scary thought, but the alternative was worse. Most people would choose to live on antibiotics with some sense of functionality as opposed to living on chemo in a wheelchair and dying early.

It seemed the logical thing was to continue on this path since I was able to keep my promise to my little girl. I was there. She had her father. And she was now attending school. By the age of four, she knew how cherished she was by me. She was beginning to understand how hard I fought for life.

But back to my MRIs…

At first I did GAD (gadolinium) contrast injections in the MRI. Then we learned it was not properly removed by my liver, so I stopped the contrast. One of my large lesions was about one inch in size. It started showing an infarct; an infarct is seen by doctors when lesions are healing. I did weekly blood work to make sure my white blood count and liver were not tanking. And I shopped around for professionals to help guide me in the world of supplements, which I knew I needed to keep detoxifying. I went to nutritionists and naturopaths without proper support. Some items they provided worked, then stopped showing results. And the costs just grew.

There was much pain and suffering when the bacteria and parasites were dying off. The healing Herxheimer reactions were ongoing, so I continued to adjust vitamin regimens to help support my body through these stresses. I was able to resume working as a regional sales representative to finally take some of the financial burden off my wife. The financial costs and lost time of being ill with a chronic illness are beyond the imagination. I have seen over 30 doctors and chiropractors. I have had many modalities, including upper cervical atlas/axis work and osteopathic cranial manipulation. My naturopathic physician relied on an EAV (electro-acupuncture according to Voll) machine to monitor my progress. The EAV readings indicated what my levels were for Borrelia, Bartonella, Mycoplasma, and other infections to provide a roadmap to target bug elimination. My bag of tricks was growing.

After several years, it became more difficult to get results from the antibiotics. My physician kept changing them up and we tried to have me take breaks from them altogether. Usually by the third day without them, I would unravel and fall apart. I always had a fuzzy crawly feeling throughout my head and body. Eventually he told me his "bag of tricks was empty." This was a terrible blow to me, but he softened the blow a little by telling me about other patients who branched out into the alternative sphere and said many of his former patients were seemingly getting favorable results with frequency therapy.

I started to read about rife machines and how they literally blow the bacteria up. It supposedly would not harm the good tissues and cells in the body, but at this point, that seemed almost irrelevant because the bugs had to make an exit. And the drug benefits were diminishing.

This was a personal choice treatment, one that is considered highly experimental in the United States. I hear that in parts of Europe, Asia, and other places it is almost standard care and not such a big deal. Here, it is considered to be a big deal to even try.

So I went to visit someone who had a GB4000 system. I call her "Chief" since she helped me by sharing her own experience and knowledge with this modality. Chief showed me her machine and how it ran. She knew I was sick, so she did not let me touch it. She only sat me next to it and ran it with the dial to the lowest possible setting. When I left, I felt energized, strong and hopeful.

A few hours later, driving home, I began having Herxheimer reactions like hell. This actually made me very hopeful and excited. I didn't enjoy any of it, but it made me happy. I purchased my own machine so I could experiment at will. The idea of being able to be in my own house with no doctor involvement and channel different frequencies into my body was intriguing. I continued the treatments on my own time schedule and loved that I could regulate the treatment based on my body's reactions, my personal work schedule, and whatever else was going on.

My head was filled with creepy crawly sensations like worms, which itched like crazy. My insomnia was unrelenting. Once in awhile I had a feeling like an elastic band popped in my head. My eyes and ears were miserable, not to mention an assortment of other reactions. In an effort to ramp up the detoxification, I purchased an infrared sauna, thousands of pounds of Epsom salt, and an insane amount of supplements. I could not afford to have my liver crap out on me. All systems were needed to clear this garbage out of my body. The infrared sauna also helped to pull heavy metals out as well. Fact: the infrared sauna penetrates the body 1.5 inches, compared to a regular sauna, which only penetrates 1/8 of an inch.

I kept pushing forward. My body was getting stronger. I started using a treadmill to strengthen my legs. I was doing more in activities in general. After many months of rife treatments, I went back to visit my Lyme literate doctor and the receptionist began to cry in joy and amazement at how well I looked. The office workers reminded me of how the third neurologist said no other treatments would ever work.

After my doctor's visit, I also stopped to visit Chief – I ran up her stairs and hugged her and twirled her around in delight!

I cannot say this treatment is easy in any way. It is very cause-and-effect oriented and sometimes the pains would stop me in my tracks, like the feeling that sharp sticks were being shoved into my swollen brain. All my old crawly tingles and burning feelings and cold wet towel on the brain feelings would resurface from time to time. But I was able to work more, and play more, and participate in my lovely growing daughter's life.

Every winter, she and I trudge through the snow and build as many snowmen as possible. Each snowfall requires its own snowman. That is our deal. We even went indoor rock climbing! I got her up and going comfortably, and then did the big wall 50-feet solo! She would guide and coach me from the ground. It felt miraculous to me. She still doesn't know how I did it! It was important to me that she saw me empowered and not a victim.

Recently, we attended an outdoor wedding and she and I danced in wild joy on a sloped grass field in the dark. I danced solid, keeping my balance and holding my daughter who is 9 years old now. I was literally able to hold her up and swing her around me, then bring her to her feet and immediately dip her back kissing her cheek. As the dance ended we walked to my wife and were stopped by a man. He asked who we were. I told him, and he responded by saying "Wow, I cannot believe what I just saw when you were dancing with your daughter. You are a lucky man. I do not get to do that with my daughter."

"Thank you," I said. "You don't know how extremely lucky I am."

I continue to treat myself. I am basically the general contractor of my own health. I have pushed for long times without any antibiotics, but have resumed them from time to time to help control the lesions. They are scary to me. When I had an MRI that showed new lesions and lesion enhancement, I pounced on the antibiotics again. I mix in anti-virals and antimicrobials as I see fit. I am diligent about detoxing and I have tried a few other modalities to try to heal up the carnage. I rife almost every day no matter what anti-whatever pills I am on or off. Most rifers cease using these pills altogether, but the lesions make my situation unique. As I said, I am the general contractor and I make my own decisions. I want to do everything I believe is necessary to ensure my survival.

All of this became my treatment for my "Lyme induced MS." I have been back in the sales workforce for the past six years. I am functioning in everyday life. I can handle multiple full days on foot through Disney heat and entertainment from Florida to California! Do I still have issues? Yes. Am I cured? No. The treatments could take years to truly eliminate the disease and allow me to fully rebuild. This is all my personal experience. I am not a doctor and I do not prescribe treatment. I am only sharing my personal story because I know what I am doing is aiding in the removing of the Lyme and co-infections that are causing havoc in my body. Sharing my story might help another person who is suffering.

The medical community is ever so slowly opening up to the disease epidemic status. Lyme disease is not something that can be cured with a week of doxycycline. If we can eliminate Lyme disease bacteria, then maybe some of the problems of MS or other manifestations can be resolved in the body. At least that is how I see it. The ability the body has to heal is unbelievable and amazing. Nerve regeneration is doable.

I am in my mid-forties now. My family has been an enormous source of support and love during this brutal journey out of my inferno and I want to thank them from the bottom of my heart! I probably would have not had the motivation and determination to triumph over death without them.

If I died tomorrow, I know my baby girl would remember me forever. I kept my promise. I am still here. She knows her father.

CALL ME ALEXANDRA

Most people give birth to their child once. I had the unfortunate – or should I say fortunate – experience of giving birth to my child twice. The original Mike up to age 14 was bogged down with physical and emotional challenges that no one could treat. It was a long, slow, downward spiral that included ADHD type behavior, rages, aches and pains, antisocial behavior, bad grades in school, and unexplained illnesses. Eventually his behavior escalated to knife grabbing, as well as suicidal and homicidal threats.

Over the past three and a half years, the "new" Mike has emerged as a sweet, caring, smart, and social (VERY social) 17-year old young man who is applying to colleges! Sometimes it is hard for me to remember his awful days, but the copious notes I took, conversations with friends I remember, and emails from teachers I saved always bring me back to reality – the reality of raising a child that I had no control over, making me feel like a bad parent. Fortunately for the "new" Mike he had a mom who was tenacious, looked at things analytically, and would never give up.

While I had twenty years of work experience in a highly charged business world, I only had two years of experience developing mommy skills with Mike's older sister. She was born two years before Mike. I was not so naive to expect he should act like his older sister, but his behavior and strange symptoms were not at all similar to a normal child his age. Something was not right. I just knew it.

Mother's intuition set in and off I went exploring different doctors, drugs, counselors, and books. And guess what? Zero answers! For a results-oriented person, I was incredibly frustrated. I felt so alone. The only common agreement there was throughout Mike's young life was that every pediatrician, psychiatrist, neurologist, psychologist, school counselor, school nurse, and teacher would say, "Yes, Mike has ADHD, but he's a puzzle."

So what does that mean? No one could answer me. There HAD to be an answer.

His early years were rough. There were constant calls and emails from teachers and counselors explaining what had happened in class that day or what Mike did to another child. I couldn't bear those emails. To think my son was disrupting the classroom or that he didn't have friends was very difficult to take. How could this have happened?

His dad and I were both smart parents. We followed all the parenting rules. We didn't allow our children to eat bad things like sugar and soda. I had a perfect pregnancy: no complications, no alcohol, no sushi, no honey, and no drugs. What was going on? During preschool we just chalked up the disruptive behavior to being a rambunctious toddler; when the symptoms started – a mild case of chicken pox and reoccurring pink eye (six times in a few months) – we thought it was due to the germs in the preschool. My antenna should have been raised when after the sixth pink eye incident and the sixth round of giving my child antibiotic eye drops each time, I finally asked my pediatrician what would he do if it was his child. He said he would take his child to a pediatric eye specialist in the city.

Why didn't he tell me that before? If I hadn't asked that question, who knows how many more times I would be pumping my little boy with antibiotics. So it was off to the specialist who told me antibiotic drops do NOTHING for pink eye. His opinion is that doctors give that to kids to make the parents think they are actually solving the problem. Supposedly pink eye just goes away on its own. This was my first foray into a world of medicine where the doctors I thought I trusted and could help me find answers was blown apart.

The next incident was when my pediatrician (a different one in the same practice) told me the only way to control my son was to hit him. WHAT??? I left that practice very quickly.

When my best mothering practices didn't work with Mike, I decided the time had come to take him to other doctors to see what was going on with him. All the doctors agreed on the same thing: Mike had ADHD and they all felt he should be on medication to control his behavior.

Off we went into the "drug my child" world so he could fit in better. We tried many different ADHD drugs, in an attempt to find one that would not make him tired or lose his appetite – all while actually controlling his symptoms. At this point the doctors had him on a steady diet of ADHD medications like Concerta or Adderall. But not knowing the long-term side effects of these Class 3 drugs always haunted me. After one of the drugs Mike tried, his eyes had big dark circles around them, almost a hollowed out look and he was more tired than usual. When I asked if the drug could be causing these symptoms, the psychiatrist compared my seven-year old son to a truck driver. "Oh he's tired like truck drivers get so that is the reason for the dark circles. You mothers always think these symptoms are from the drugs."

Again – WHAT??? Did I just hear these condescending remarks? Now I was more frightened than ever about what I was putting into my son's body. I left this doctor, too.

Slowly but surely I was losing my faith in these professionals. We did find a more empathetic psychiatrist and a medicine that somewhat worked. At least for awhile. But it seemed sporadic. Some days it worked and some it didn't. We added another drug to help the other drug work better. I had conflicting feelings but they clearly gave me a period of relief and a calmer home environment. I have no idea what it did for him because he had difficulty articulating anything clearly.

There were other moms I spoke with who had kids with ADHD, but they didn't seem to mind drugging their children. I live in an area where so many kids are medicated that it has become almost generally accepted. But it bothered me. And I was bothered that other parents weren't bothered. Other moms just told me to keep quiet and not tell anyone that my son had "issues." But I wanted the world to know what was going on with my son so maybe, just maybe, someone could help my son! If I kept quiet then I was perpetuating the idea that mental illness is something you don't talk about and if you ignore it, it will go away. So I talked and talked and talked to people and asked question after question until I found answers I could work with that could help improve Mike's life.

By the time Mike was a preteen, we were constantly battling bad behavior and his inability/unwillingness to do school work. A typical day went like this:

"Mike, time to get up!"

In most homes, this phrase would signal the start of a day of activity. Not in our home. For many years it would become a battle cry marking the beginning of an hour-long struggle to get my son out of bed, washed up, dressed, fed, and through the door to meet the bus at the corner. Most times the simple task of wrestling him out of bed would fray my nerves and result in shouting and browbeating. And this was just the start of the day.

Many days would end the same way. The battle over homework would often end with fruitless ranting and empty threats to withhold favors in the future. Frustration and impatience are two words that describe my efforts to keep Mike on task for school. Here was a boy who could recite lines of dialogue from films that he had seen years ago but would not – or at least we thought he would not rather than could not – commit the simplest fact to memory. We would drill him from the study guides for tests until he could give back all the information on the guides. The painful effort seemed worth it. Then on review the next morning, it would all be gone – what was "known" at 9pm the night before was lost by the time he took the tests.

Through this entire time there was a sense that he was willfully resisting learning simply because we were pushing him so hard. So in response to this assumption, we pushed harder and harder. As I think back on those years, I am embarrassed to think of the pain we must have caused him. I know now that the affliction that attacked him physically since he was a toddler also affected his ability to process information. The constant pressure to "do it our way" made

Mike believe that he was slow and couldn't succeed in school.

In retrospect, those years were marked with constant conflict. Resistance greeted every chore, every household task, and every school assignment. Stop watching TV, wrap up your video game, get ready for bed, pick up your clothes, unload your backpack – all directives were met with resistance, which in turn was met by frustration, which eventually led to anger. I can say that after many of these encounters, I would be overcome by feelings of guilt and inadequacy. What kind of parent continuously battles with their son over the most minor things?

He would be lost in a video game for hours on end, or texting for more hours on end. Entire afternoons and evenings were spent watching the same movies over and over and over again. This was Mike's social life for many years. Friends? He had one guy who shared his interest in video games and street hockey but when that companion was busy, he had no one else his age to hang out with.

We knew the reasons why he made kids uncomfortable. Mike seemed to lack a sense of social boundaries. When we saw him in groups he would stand uncomfortably close and would roughhouse regardless of the reactions of others. He would either talk incessantly or be unnaturally quiet. He was unable to develop a level of trust with other boys or girls in his grades and only seemed comfortable with family and other adults. One of the reasons for his spotty school attendance in middle school and in the first few years of high school was his feeling that no one liked him.

Although most of his teachers saw Mike as a smart, witty kid, they recognized his problems with his peers. On birthdays we struggled to find kids to invite to his parties, which ended up being family events. Our advice throughout this time was to encourage him to be more outgoing and sensitive to how his behavior was affecting those around him. Think of it. We were advising a 13-year old to just be more sensitive, to just be nicer. How useless and hollow those words seem in retrospect.

More and more physical symptoms started to emerge, like fatigue, achy joints, stomach aches, and now those dark circles appeared all the time. Something was clearly amiss more than a mental issue. As a preteen, Mike was still wetting his bed several times a week. It was heartbreaking to have a child that age having to sleep in Pull-Ups. It was exhausting to constantly wash sheets and pajamas, and impossible to keep him from feeling ashamed. The ramifications of trying to not make him feel ashamed and not being able to sleep at other kids homes was difficult. I was worried that he would be like this the rest of his life.

As miserable as I was, I knew I had a very unhappy child who was very miserable himself. I began to wonder if he knew what "normal" felt like. When I would ask him how he felt, he would answer that he didn't know. Or if I would yell at him – oh how hard I tried not to yell – he would just look at me and say, "Mom I can't help it. I have ADHD." I wanted to cry.

Everything started to escalate. His rage and frustrations were out of control and the household starting falling apart. On some occasions he would grab a kitchen knife; his sister would lock herself in her room. (And on occasion I would, too!) If something didn't go Mike's way or he couldn't figure something out quickly, he would immediately go into a rage. Throw things, scream, run after me. One time he pushed me so hard I fell down a step. Many times he ran outside as if to run away, but fortunately he never did that. He would get so frustrated he would lock himself into the bathrooms, my bedroom, his sister's bedroom, or his bedroom. I could not get him out no matter what I tried, and got scared when he didn't answer me. Was he planning on hurting himself? Finally I had to take the locks off of all rooms with the exception of his sister's bedroom because she needed a safe place to escape. How awful is it when you don't feel safe in your own home?

At another doc visit Mike was diagnosed with yet another ailment: borderline Oppositional Defiant Disorder. ODD is a condition in which a child displays an ongoing pattern of uncooperative, defiant, hostile, and annoying behavior towards people in authority. The child's behavior often disrupts the child's normal daily activities, including activities within the family and at school. Do you know what that could mean if this gets worse when he is a teenager? It could lead to drug or alcohol addiction or other dangerous acts. I knew if I didn't intervene soon he could end up an addict, in jail, or worse.

Mike's elementary school tried to be as supportive as they could be. They gave him a 504 plan and some special services. One specialist who was helping Mike with writing skills diagnosed him with Sensory Processing Disorder, a condition that exists when multisensory integration is not adequately processed in order to provide appropriate responses to the demands of the environment. Mike's was more of an auditory input issue resulting in inattentiveness, disorganization, and poor school performance. If the room was noisy he could not concentrate, so very often he would go to other quiet rooms to take tests. One evening we went with a crowd to an ice hockey game and as everyone was standing and cheering he would sit there with his hands over his ears. We had to leave early.

Very few people, even close friends, knew how difficult it was day to day. I often felt when I would tell friends the details of how Mike acted it sounded trivial, but it was the culmination of these behaviors day in and day out that made it so difficult and exhausting. Most kids at some point throw tantrums and misbehave, but it is balanced out with good behavior. The good behavior should outweigh the bad behavior. For Mike, there was virtually no semblance of good behavior. Just bad behavior or general suffering.

I had always wanted children and knew the "rules" of motherhood. To protect, provide, and do ANYTHING to keep your child safe, happy, educated, and healthy. I was failing on all counts. If I was working for a company I would have been fired. At baby showers, all you hear is how lucky you are and how amazing your life will be with a child. No one tells you about potential struggles of NOT having the perfect child or, God forbid, a sick child. So where was I to turn? There were times in my life where I failed but I could not afford this to be one of those times.

At this point I started to believe there was something more complicated going on with my son. Yes, he had ADHD symptoms. But why? I started to search for missing pieces and explanations. I investigated our well water, mold, food sensitivities, and toxic chemicals. I was convinced there was something more. There had to be. I wanted Mike to go to college – although at this rate I would be happy if he just graduated high school and made one more friend.

A few years later, as we were trying to enjoy our first trip abroad together as a family, I started developing strange rashes all over my body. I was achy and incredibly tired. Hard to know where to go in a foreign country, but I knew France had good medical care so the first stop was a pharmacist. "Spider bites," the pharmacist said in broken English. "Use this cream and all will be fine." What a relief!

A few days later, though, as I was getting ready to go to the Louvre, the right side of my face was paralyzed. I couldn't smile, close my right eye, or drink from a glass. So it was off to a Paris hospital where they diagnosed me with Lyme disease and Bells Palsy.

Lyme disease? We had a ton of deer in my backyard so maybe that is where I got bit. I called my doctor's office in the United States to get an appointment as soon as I returned home so I could be prescribed the typical three weeks of doxycycline. (France only prescribes amoxycillin.) The nurse on the phone, however, told me it was not Lyme disease because you do not get Bells Palsy from Lyme. After doing some research in the medical community, Bells Palsy is one of the flagship symptoms of Lyme disease.

There is a lot of controversy in the Lyme disease world, but Bells Palsy is not one of them. Another clueless medical professional.

As my journey to cure myself began, I read and watched whatever I could to understand why after 3 weeks of doxycycline I started to get new symptoms. I thought 3 to 4 weeks of doxycycline would cure me. The docs said it would. But I started getting knee pain. First on the right side, then on the left; it would migrate from knee to knee. This was no classic symptom of a sports injury or arthritis.

A tennis friend whose daughter was very sick with Lyme disease told me I had to watch a documentary called "Under Our Skin." I immediately picked it up and watched the two-hour horror story of lives completely changed by Lyme disease. I cried and vowed that I would NEVER let myself get as sick as these people and that I would do whatever I could to make sure of that. This movie changed my life and my perspective on diseases and the medical community.

So I joined a support group and began learning from and helping others understand and deal with Lyme disease. In this process, I found an interesting article about pediatric Lyme disease. I never thought about my own child having Lyme disease or anyone else in my family, but as I read the article the list of common symptoms hit me like a ton of bricks. Lack of focus, inattentiveness, irritability, memory issues, uncontrollable behavior, rages, and fidgeting are all Lyme disease symptoms. Was this the missing piece? This was my second turning point.

Meanwhile, I had been on a waiting list for the "Best Lyme Doc" in the area and one of the best in the country. These physicians are commonly referred to as Lyme Literate Doctors or LLMDs. This doctor was medically trained at a prestigious hospital and treated hundreds of patients. Eight months? Are you kidding me? Wow, this doctor must be incredible to have such a long waitlist – and they only treat patients with Lyme disease. I would wait. After five months I got the call: "We have an opening in two weeks. Would you like it?" Of course I would!

I will be well soon, I thought, and back on the tennis court with no pain. During my first two-hour appointment, the doctor felt very strongly I had Lyme disease and that my symptoms from eight years prior were from Lyme disease as well – but they still needed to do blood work to confirm which tick-borne diseases I had so they could develop a more specific protocol for me. I tested positive for Lyme Borrelia, Rocky Mountain Spotted Fever, Mycoplasma and Ehrlichia.

Eight years earlier, when Mike was still an infant, I had just stopped nursing him when I got a very bad sinus infection. The first sinus infection in my life that resulted in a temporary loss of smell and taste and then headaches, fatigue, reoccurring yeast infections, and nausea. My physician at that time ran blood tests and ultimately diagnosed me with stress. She told me to quit my job, so I did. I believed her diagnosis. I had two small children in preschool, a full-time high-stress job that required me to travel occasionally, and a husband who travelled all the time. No one suggested I get tested for Lyme disease.

I live in a state that is one of the leading states for Lyme, so why do doctors and pediatricians rarely consider Lyme as a possibility? (Could this be considered malpractice?) These bugs were festering in my body for years, spreading throughout every organ. Who knows what long-term effects I will have. I had trusted my practitioners.

Back to my appointment with my leading LLMD. During that first appointment, I asked them about Mike, even though I had never found a bulls-eye rash on him. I think we may have pulled a tick or two off of him when he was young, but it was not something I really thought about at that time. Now I felt this was something worth looking into. The doctor seemed certain that he had Lyme disease, so we scheduled an appointment shortly thereafter for him.

While we waited for the appointment date, I decided to go to

Mike's pediatrician and get his blood work done for the ELISA and Western Blot tests. I had learned through the support group that the standard test for Lyme disease, the ELISA, was very unreliable and that we should have the Western Blot test done at the same time. (This test is unreliable as well, but more accurate than the ELISA.) Both came back negative.

At Mike's first LLMD appointment, more blood was drawn; this was sent off to a specialty lab in California, IGenex, which had a more reliable and specific testing method. $2100 later the testing came back positive for Borrelia and Bartonella. I finally found my missing piece! I was invigorated. Let's get my baby boy cured and me too!

I was in good hands and I thought my LLMD was the answer to my prayers. My "follow the rules" German upbringing guided me throughout this process. Mike and I both religiously went to see this doctor every two months for three years; I frequently pulled him out of school or from activities so he could see the doctor and do WHATEVER they said. We started off with some meds and supplements, then blood tests, stool tests, biofilm tests, EKG's. We ran allergy tests – he was allergic to cow dairy (casein), basil (included in most tomato sauces), honey, cherries, chocolate, and xanthan gum (in almost all chewing gums). It was difficult having a twelve-year old not being able to eat the mainstay of every school and birthday party: pizza and brownies. And I was told that artificial sugar could only worsen his symptoms.

We finally found the right goat milk, goat yogurt, goat cream cheese, and goat cheese that he could eat and actually liked! And don't get me started on chewing gums. Every chewing gum has an artificial sweetener in it, even if it isn't sugar free, except Glee Gum, which is hard to find. And most have xanthan gum. I went to the extremes of buying him a Make it Yourself Glee Gum Kit for Christmas so he could feel better about him being the ONLY one not being allowed to chew Big League Chew or Juicy Fruit. What a sticky mess!

This poor child! What was I doing to Mike? He was not getting better AND he was still on Concerta. The laundry list of meds and supplements started to grow: Artemesian, Betaine, Daytrana, Concerta, Alinia, A-L Complex, A-Bart, SyCircue, SyImmune, Burbur, Parsley, Nystatin, Cilantro, A-BAB, Methylphenidate, Probiotics, A-V, Itires, Intuniv, Plant Enzymes, Amoxycillin, Serrapeptase, Renelix, Vitamin D3, Phosperine DHA, Thorne Trace Minerals, vitamin B12, Thorne Iso-Phos, Protect 120 Lotion, Golden Thread Supreme, BAB2, Thorne Heavy Metal Support, SyAllgen, Lymph Tone II, Interface Plus, Diflucan, Krill oil, NeproRella/Chlorella, Xymogen Lotion, Cumanda, Boluoke, Zithromax, Perque C Guard, Perque, Ceftin, BaCoFlor, EndoSupreme, Coenzyme B, Melserdazale, Milk Thistle, Biotin 8, Ultimate E, Health Genesis, Erythromycin, Prescript Assist, Ketek, Mycelia, SyCrest, Omnicef, Drainage Tone, Vaccin-Chord, Melia Supreme, Minocin, GPC Choline, Inflammar, Houttuynia, DigestZyme and I'm sure I left out a few. Every day a pile of pills was laid out for him. Fortunately he didn't complain except when he had to take Ceftin, a horse-sized pill that we found went down easier when coated with butter. Funny though that his 86-year old grandmother would complain about her taking eight pills a day, which was nothing compared to Mike.

Astoundingly, despite our religious commitment to this LLMD, and following medical orders precisely, during this three-year period, Mike's symptoms started to grow.

In addition to those mentioned previously, he had dizziness when standing, red dotted streaks on his back and shoulder, aches in back of leg, wrists, shins, back, elbows, shoulder blades, ankles, kneecaps hurt while running, legs throbbed, blurry spots when reading, bottom of foot burned, red cheeks, stiff neck, shivering, sweating at night, white blisters under lower lip, felt like a worm was crawling in his eyes, his hands, feet and knees were swollen, ringing in ears, heart pounding, headaches, nauseous, red itchy patches, sad, gassy, fishy breath, hands throb and swollen, itchy eyes, ulcers on tongue, trouble breathing after exercise, ear hurt. And one of the worst for me: incessant talking. He could NOT stop talking, and usually not nice things would come out of his mouth. I wanted so much to tell him to "shut up" but I didn't allow him to say that so how could I? It would drive me crazy. Another reason I would lock myself in my bedroom. Most of these symptoms were not at the same time, but they all occurred frequently.

At every appointment, the doctor would say to me that Mike was getting better. At first, I was so confused, but I bought into her analysis. Maybe he was herxing or maybe a new layer of bugs was emerging or maybe he got bit again. I was learning more and more about this disease and every time I thought I had a handle on it this LLMD threw me for a loop. "Mike is getting better," they said. "But we need more information so let's get blood work done to see if he has food allergies" or "let's get stool samples done to see if he has parasites" or "let's do blood work to see if he has the 'new' FL1953." Oh, and you live in an old house so you should do mold remediation. Eat organic, eat only sprouted breads, don't eat dairy or wheat, no sugar, take a probiotic. The list was endless, but my pocketbook wasn't.

How do you choose which tests, medicines, or other doctors to see on a limited budget? None of this is covered by insurance. Lyme disease is a "rich man's" disease. Make sure you are rich before you get this disease or else you are screwed.

So how did I decide what to do? Remember I said I would do ANYTHING to help my child. This was my job and my unwritten oath. I had to do whatever I could to get him well. So I did it all.

At one point, his rage and wanting to kill himself got so bad I spoke with a few therapists who said I need to take these threats seriously and I should take him to a pediatric psychiatric clinic. Reluctantly, we took him there for an evaluation. A psychiatrist evaluated him and she didn't think he needed to be admitted, but it was up to us. We decided not to admit him. Once you admit someone they need to stay for at least a week and I couldn't handle having him alone in there for a week without contact with his parents at the age of 12. (I learned later that the evaluator herself was having major psychological problems and had been on leave and was now on probation. Again my intuition said do not admit him. I thought the whole evaluation process was odd). I would come to realize that this was a very wise decision.

What about therapy? Yes that's the answer! We had done some therapy years ago when Mike was young, but I didn't think it helped much. Now that he was older, though, maybe it could. Behavioral therapy will help Mike change this time. We found a very kind, knowledgeable psychologist who also had Lyme disease. Our whole family went to see her. At this time we were all a mess. The stress was getting unbearable and my marriage was falling apart.

My husband was also diagnosed with Lyme disease (if one spouse has Lyme, almost always the other has it, too – it's like its closest relative syphilis) and his rage was getting out of control. He was also diagnosed with Bartonella and Borrelia.

Two raging, out of control people in the house was more than I could handle. In fact, it was also more than the psychologist could handle. After a few months she honestly said she could not help us any longer. What I did not realize at the time was that the Lyme disease bugs were controlling my son's brain and no therapy would help him. It was not Mike resisting me at every turn but those damn bugs! No wonder all those techniques in those behavior books didn't work. He literally couldn't control his own thinking or behavior! All that time and money spent on talk therapy was a huge waste. Perhaps it helped me a bit as I thought I was doing something rather than nothing and it did let me vent a little. Maybe I was a better mom than I thought!

My approach to mothering Mike changed. I stopped punishing him for things I believed he could not control. We helped him understand that he was not bad, but it was the bugs controlling his behavior. When he began to get healthier I think I did a good job of convincing him of that. When he would do something wrong he would look at me and say "Mom, but I have ADHD AND Lyme Disease." At least he made me laugh at times. We tried to get him to better articulate how he felt both physically and emotionally, but at this stage of his disease it was useless.

After three years and tens of thousands of dollars, I called it quits with our LLMD. I give LLMDs a lot of credit for attempting to tackle this disease. They are certainly excellent at diagnosing tick-borne illnesses, but to the best of my knowledge they have no cures. Some patients may get better or perhaps their disease is being managed, but for me and Mike we did not see any improvement. Mike was not getting better and I honestly believe he got worse.

In our final months with the LLMD, I had started exploring alternative methods to treat our Lyme and co-infections. It was scary to leave an "expert" in their field and go off in a different direction. Maybe we all would have been worse off without this doctor. Who knows? Who was going to guide me?

I was invited to a luncheon with six other woman who all had Lyme disease or had children who were infected. I kept hearing a woman at the end of the table tell another woman, "Instead of going on another round of IV antibiotics, have you considered a rife machine?" I had heard about this machine before but didn't hear good things. Nonetheless, I wanted to know more and couldn't help ignoring those around me and listening to the conversation at the other end of the table. This woman with the rife machine felt she would have died if not for this machine. The last time I had heard that something was so effective for Lyme disease was when I was told antibiotics would cure us. HA! That didn't happen.

Yet, after the lunch, I went home and researched this machine. I called this woman at the end of the table and I went to her house to speak with her. My first words to her were, "My son is 13 and I have 5 years to get him well. Do you think he could get results with this modality?" (I figured I may not have much control over what Mike did when he reached 18 and I wanted him to go to college.) She reminded me of all I had tried already, which did not work, and said this would be worth a try. So I started my journey into the alternative world.

Alternative modalities were not something I had really been exposed to or understood before. I had always thought of them as 'voodoo' medicine. I tried the frequency machine a few times and I had herx reactions. And often, the day after I rifed, I would feel really good. I remember trying to time my rife sessions the day before a tennis match so I would have energy and less pain on the court. More research and talking to others convinced me this was an investment I had to make.

I decided to buy my own machine and see if Mike could improve without medications. With support from my new best friend and whatever research I could get my hands on, I dove right in. We started very gradually and experienced healing reactions. Within three weeks, my son's face blew up like the Elephant Man's and brown toxins began pouring out of his front gums, which tasted like rotten eggs. What had I done? I called old doctors and dentists, new doctors and dentists, and they all said the toxins coming out were actually a good sign. I came to find out that a front teeth injury he had in 2nd grade was harboring bacteria, probably Lyme disease spirochetes, and the rife machine killed that bacteria and the toxins needed a place to escape. Better out than in.

Toxins in the bloodstream can be deadly. I thought Mike would lose his two injured front teeth, but luckily he didn't. What a powerful machine! This was his first of many intense and mild healing reactions.

Kill the bugs, feel crummy, then get a bit better. We cautiously continued rifing, but I felt we needed to add some other modalities to support the killing of bacteria, parasites, viruses, protozoa, etc. Killing was one thing, but supporting and boosting the immune system was something else. Again, I researched and was overwhelmed with the options available in this new form of medicine. Of course, few things are approved by the FDA or AMA so I had to seek out others opinions, attend presentations, research online, and again go on gut instinct.

On the opinion of another friend, I was introduced to a holistic practitioner who could help clear the toxins from Mike's body and provide nutritional supplements where there were clear deficits. With his help, Mike seemed to bounce back more quickly from the rife sessions; the doctor also helped Mike get off of his ADHD medications. This was a huge deal for me. Remember I was very nervous about the long-term effects of the ADHD medications. Now I knew that his ADHD symptoms were a manifestation of the Lyme disease. We started rifing in April when Mike was in 8th grade, and by the end of June that year he had taken his LAST ADHD pill! There were times over that summer that I wanted him to pop a pill again, but I knew that ingesting one potential poison while killing others was not a step forward. I had to keep marching on. No looking back.

By this time I felt more confident in leaving my LLMD. Since Mike's last appointment in March I had only contacted this doctor once to get their opinion on the Elephant Man syndrome. I was still a mess and frustrated as to why Mike couldn't get healthier more quickly and why there was no one guiding me through this hell hole. It was now Mike's 9th grade, his first year of high school. He had to get well quickly so he could get back on track academically. I knew his healing reactions could be bad and intense during that first year of rifing, but I had no idea how difficult it would be. Missing 42 days of school was not a way to start off. The killing of these bugs would set him back that year, but I kept being reminded that you have to kill those bugs before you can begin to heal. The longer you wait the more intense those bugs will get. I had to get them out of his body and do it fast.

I began to rife him more aggressively that first year. I continued to lean on the holistic practitioner to ensure Mike was getting the right nutritional support. I steeped Mike in six pounds of an Epsom salt bath every week to help him get rid of these toxins. Another trip to Costco to buy my truckloads of Dr. Teal's Epsom Salt.

There are conflicting opinions on how hard to push someone when you are using frequencies to try to kill bugs. There is not a set protocol on how to do this. It is part science and part art. I tried to schedule his 'killing" sessions so he wouldn't miss too many school activities and obligations. College was fast approaching and I was feeling a lot of pressure to have him perform well enough academically so maybe he could even apply to college.

It was so easy to get bogged down in the everyday minutiae of suburbia competition. All his classmates were getting into Honors and AP classes, doing community work, getting involved in church groups or foreign language classes, or participating in multiple afterschool activities. I was lucky if Mike was able to get up on his own and go to school at all! I kept having to put my life in perspective and realize the ONLY important thing was to get my son healthy. And not just feeling better. I wanted ALL of those damn bugs out of him. NOW!

I was worried Mike would be missing critical information his freshman year and that he would get far behind. It was very rough, but with the help of his teachers and counselor he made it through. Only one teacher was not on board and thought Mike's now only occasional disruptive behavior was Mike's way of annoying the teacher on purpose. He could not understand that Lyme disease or ADHD could do this. I finally got him on the phone and shifted how I approached him. I told him Mike had a brain infection and he sometimes had no control over what he said or did. That helped a little, but the teacher was never completely on board. I am grateful for those professionals who were supportive through our ordeal.

At this point I began to see concrete results. The bedwetting was getting less and less, his rage was not as intense, and his physical symptoms started to diminish. I started to see windows of hope and my comfort level with being on my own and using these modalities started to grow. I really felt I was giving rebirth to the child I know today. It was the first time I really felt hopeful and I knew the original Mike would be replaced by a new Mike who could be whole and a normally functioning person in society. I knew I had a long way to go and I was willing to consider additional modalities to add into my new arsenal. I was willing to embrace anything that resonated with me.

One presentation that truly had an impact on me was an upper cervical chiropractor. I had never heard of this specialty, but the presentation seemed to make so much sense. Straighten out your body so your brain and body can function properly to improve your immune system. I made an appointment the next morning and this time had Mike be the guinea pig. After his first adjustment, he herxed! Odd to think a mom is so excited that her son is getting sick for a day or two, but I knew he was healing in the long term. Mike would sleep for sixteen hours a day in response to the treatment. He seemed to be getting better and better. Symptoms gradually started going away and even a Doctor of Osteopathy, a DO, who we had been seeing for about a year who performed cranial sacral treatments saw a huge shift in Mike's brain! I thought I was on the right path.

Fortunately the DO we were seeing was very holistic and suggested Mike consider acupuncture to unblock whatever was blocked. This time I bagged the research (so tired of researching modalities) because I actually trusted this doc. Mike was a bit apprehensive about getting needles stuck in him but he was a real trooper. In fact, Mike was a real trooper throughout most of this process. He rarely bucked me on going to docs or taking his medications, maybe because he trusted me or maybe because I didn't give him a choice. There was no choice. When I made up my mind he HAD to do it. Mike had needles stuck in his ears, forehead, chest, arms, legs, feet, almost everywhere. Some of them hurt but most didn't. Even short-term permanent ones in his ear. He thought that was cool when he went to school with earrings! To help his brain and the emotional toll this disease was taking on Mike, the DO performed the 7 dragons treatment. This is an Ancient Chinese treatment where needles are set in a pattern that reconnect the patient to themselves, in essence expelling the 7 demons that can take over your body. I prefer to think of it more like it engages the Qi (energy) in your body.

As we were ending the first year of Mike's rebirth, my new Mike started to emerge. Sometimes I couldn't even believe the remarkable changes. He smiled more, and the emails stopped coming from school. In fact, he wasn't even on their radar at all and his 504 was rarely being used. Calls from friends started coming, the dinnertime conversations were positive and not a barrage of silly obnoxious behavior. I noticed on vacation that he and his sister were in the pool having a great time whereas in the past they would constantly fight. I put the locks back on the doors and the knives back in the drawers. I noticed his physical appearance changed and he started growing and thriving. He began to notice the world around him in a way he couldn't before. I remember the first time he said to me "I feel happy!" He began to talk rationally to me and his humor started to come out. He was always a bit of a jokester but the ADHD medication would stifle that. I remember my brother once saying at an Easter dinner, "I like Mike better off his medication because he is funnier." Mike now is almost TOO funny. He is always joking and engaging in adult humor, which can be very witty. And gone are the days that he could not tolerate loud noises . There are times now I wish he were a little more sound sensitive – he blasts Uptown Funk and sings wildly every chance he can get! It was like an archaeological dig: as we kept excavating and peeling back layers of his illness, the new and exciting Mike started to emerge.

We are nearly four years into this alternative journey and Mike is an entirely different child. He went from having no friends to lots of friends, from missing 42 days of school his freshman year to barely missing any days now, from being on ADHD medicine every day since 2nd grade to nothing by the end of 8th grade, from not being able to sit in a classroom without disrupting behavior to sitting in an ACT testing room for hours taking the tests and doing really well, from constantly having all kinds of symptoms to almost nothing! And it has been three years since he wet the bed! His behavior for a 17-year old still has much to be desired, but he has turned into a lovable, caring, smart, much calmer teenager. All without medication!

This journey has been life altering for my family. I learned many lessons and learned to evaluate people much better than I had before. I learned that the medical community does NOT have all the answers and blind faith in them did NOT serve us well. Some docs I speak with are open to what I have done, but many just give me a questioning look and probably think I have been taken for a ride by some quacks.

The results don't lie. We are all happier and healthier and in a strange way closer. I could never understand why Mike would say "I hate my life" or why he was so angry and would not listen to reason. I realized that no matter how much therapy, or medications, or timeouts we imposed, or having things being taken away from him, his behavior was not changing. The bugs had taken over his body and brain and they were doing the talking. I had to get that bug load down before he could change his behavior. All those strategies in child behavior books just didn't work. But alternative modalities did!

This experience has also changed the way I look at the outside world. We can no longer enjoy rolling in the autumn leaves, taking hikes though the woods, or camping outside. The risk of getting re-infected from a tick bite is just too high. Even the simple things of taking Prom pictures in the grass or playing Frisbee on the lawn makes me freak out. If we cannot avoid the grass, we spray our clothes and skin and do immediate tick checks. The adorable deer that roam our backyard are now met with distain. When I see children crawling through brush or running into the woods to retrieve a ball, I cringe. Those ticks are not discriminatory. They will bite whoever crosses their path and leave behind their devastation. Yet, most people and medical practitioners don't understand the ramifications of Lyme disease and other tick-borne infections. That's why I had to go it alone.

Or should I say with some dear non-medically trained friends who helped me navigate the most intense experience of my life.

The doctors failed me, politicians failed me, and even my marriage failed me. But some friends did not. I am grateful to have my new Mike, a wonderful young man less disabled by illness who can now enjoy life as it was meant to be enjoyed.

Lately I've been helping friends help their children navigate this Lyme world. The words I seem to keep repeating are:

You can't do this alone. You need support from friends and medical practitioners who at least somewhat understand this disease.

There is a consensus that it takes five years to heal. We don't want to just feel better. We want to be healed.

"You can't rationalize with irrational people." When dealing with neurological issues the bugs do the talking – not the person. And those bugs can say the craziest things.

Keep asking questions. There is never a dumb question. When you're done asking questions, ask another. Disease is NOT the new normal.

I wish that every mother out there who has a child with an ADHD or ODD diagnosis would not automatically surrender to the medical establishment and their protocols. Talk to other parents, research on your own, try other protocols, and most importantly DON'T GIVE UP! Use that mother's intuition and the internet to see if there is a better solution for your child. In my dozens of conversations with parents over these past few years, I've learned that so many children have all kinds of symptoms that seem to have become the "new" normal. I constantly hear parents tell me their teenagers have in addition to ADHD symptoms, anxiety, depression, suicidal thoughts, eating disorders, stomach problems, migraines, reoccurring sinus infections, fibroids, severe menstrual cramps, joint pain, Crohn's disease, Colitis, Celiac disease, and allergies to everything! My daughter told me that there is not one person she knows at college who is NOT on a prescribed medication! What kind of society are we raising? There has to be other solutions.

Tomorrow, we are sending out all of Mike's college applications. Five years ago, I never thought he would be here, but the hard work and never giving up has brought us to a point every mother wants: to have a healthy, happy, smart, caring child who is ready for the adult world. Am I ready to send him off to college? Yes I am! But I am sure his laundry will return home with the excuse of "But Mom I have ADHD and Lyme Disease!" To which I will reply, "Not any more!"

I can think of no more fitting person to conclude this story than Mike, who recounted his own escape from the Lyme inferno in his college essay – an essay that brought his guidance counselor to tears and sent goose bumps up and down her arms.

"I love it," she wrote me. "What a success story Mike is. I am so glad to have known him these three plus years and seen these changes in him. I wouldn't change a thing."

Of course, when she said "I wouldn't change a thing," she was talking about editing the essay any further. I would have changed so many things about Mike's life. I wish he would have never been sick. I wish he could have always known health and happiness.

But in light of reality, I am so proud that my boy – my son reborn – was finally able to share all of his feelings as he takes the next steps in his life journey:

I am a different person now. Up until my junior year, it seemed as if I went through the school day in a fog. I know what it feels like to be left out. When a teacher calls out a classmate for blurting out something stupid or not paying attention, most classmates will roll their eyes and snicker. I just think to myself, "I've been there."

I used to be afraid of just about everything, always anxious about the day ahead of me. I felt like I was not wanted in the world and that nobody would care if I was gone. It was not that I was "bullied" as much as I always thought that I was an outsider. Kids did not like me very much. They thought I was weird and annoying and awkward. It was impossible for me to focus or concentrate, and I would often disrupt class with less than brilliant remarks. My sister was even embarrassed by me, so she ignored me when I said "hi" to her in the hallways at school. She did not know what it was like to be me.

I did not know who to trust. Other than my mother and father, there was only one person in my life who stayed by my side: my friend, Jonathan. It was almost impossible for me to do anything on my own. Everything was an argument. There was never a moment of quiet in my house. I never got out of bed in the morning without forcing my mom or dad to yell or threaten. During my freshman year, I missed almost a quarter of the school year due to illness, and I did not care about myself or my grades. My life was a big mess. It was pretty miserable. I did not know what it was like to feel normal when people told me that I was not behaving like a normal kid. The hardest part of those years was that I really wanted to be like the kids that I admired in school. I just could not do it. But I guess people change – because I changed.

Starting Lyme disease treatment changed my life. I had visited dozens of doctors over the years. I had taken medications too numerous to count, and eventually my mom and I hit on something that worked, and I began to get healthier. The turning point was in the summer before my sophomore year. My grades began improving and I became more social. I began feeling that my teachers really liked me. Other kids were seeking me out to be their friend. I had never experienced this before. It felt fantastic.

It became easier to wake up in the morning for school because I really wanted to go, and homework was not as hard for me. I could concentrate and listen better, and I was involved in class discussions without disrupting the class with silly comments. I was much happier with myself and gained confidence. I thought about my past life and why I used to be the way that I was. Why I used to think that I was not needed in the world. It was not that I was a "bad" or "stupid" person. It was because my head and body were filled with a disease that controlled who I was and how I felt.

Even though Lyme made me pretty miserable, I realize that many other people are suffering as well. I know this battle has made me a more empathetic person. I can now relate better to those who struggle, especially those with cognitive issues. Now, I am the one who invites the unwanted kids to sit at my lunch table. I am now on the right track, academically and socially, and I am ready to take the next step. I used to dread thinking about the future. Not anymore.

CALL ME ANN

What follows is my arduous journey through Lyme and tick-borne diseases. Looking back, I cannot believe I survived it. The road was filled with so much pain, anguish, and despair. Only by the grace of God and my wonderful family was I able to endure it. Along the way, I met some of the greatest, most caring, and selfless people I have ever known.

At the age of fifteen, I came down with a huge rash on my back. The rash was red and purple and was in streaks across my entire back. It looked like I had sat against an old time radiator with the slats long enough to burn my skin. My parents, being very concerned, took me from doctor to doctor. A blood test showed that I had a positive ANA count, which is usually associated with an autoimmune condition. I was not displaying any other symptoms at this time, but the rash persisted. Some doctors thought I might have Lupus, but I did not have any of the other markers that are associated with the disease. The rash eventually faded, but my ANA blood test – which measures the wellbeing of my autoimmune system – would stay positive for many years.

During the next twenty years I lived a pretty normal life. I completed college, got married, and moved to California with my husband. I worked hard during this time, going back to school to earn my teaching credentials and complete student teaching. We returned to the East Coast and I started working as a teacher. It was a job I loved, but it also had me on my feet all day. It was in these years that my mystery illnesses began to surface.

I came down with horrible urinary pain, gut wrenching stomach pain, and painful joints. I went to numerous doctors and had many tests performed but everything always came back negative. My parents were very hard working people and instilled in me that work ethic. I pushed through the symptoms, continued to work, and chalked up my symptoms to growing older.

In 2007, after taking time off to raise my children, I started teaching again full-time. I completed my first year at an amazing school and was gearing up for the following school year when my life fell apart. I woke up one morning in July 2008 with my face paralyzed. I could not smile or close my eye. I went to the emergency room and had many tests performed. After five hours I was released, with the diagnosis of a viral infection. I left without much worry, figuring this would go away. Considering I already had a myriad of other persisting symptoms throughout my life, I do not know why I had such naïve optimism.

Things only continued to get worse during the next several days. The paralysis of my face continued and my thinking became muddled. It felt like someone had twisted my brain and I was trying to think through that. I developed the worst headache pain I have ever had and it was unrelenting. This pain would stay with me for the next four years.

My arms and legs became numb and I had shooting stabs of electric sensations running through them. I became exhausted to the point where I had to stay in bed. Back I went to a different emergency room where numerous tests were performed, including a spinal tap to rule out meningitis. But, again, the tests came back negative. I knew someone who had Lyme disease and I discussed the possibility of this being the reason for my symptoms with the doctors evaluating me. A Lyme test was performed and I was sent on my way with a prescription for Doxycycline, a standard protocol for Lyme disease.

This would be the first of a seemingly endless list of drugs prescribed to me in the years to come. Allow me to keep track throughout my story.

#1 Doxycycline

At this point, I knew deep down that something was seriously wrong with me. I wasn't bouncing back like I had always done with previous illnesses. My symptoms were intensifying and my mental capacity was deteriorating rapidly. I thought that my head symptoms would disappear as my bell's palsy dissipated, but it didn't. My thinking became more and more cloudy and my memory became horrible. If someone spoke to me, it would take up to three minutes for my mind to comprehend it and formulate a response. It was like trying to think through syrup. My eyes became extremely painful and light sensitive. My response to sounds was so hypersensitive that any sound shot through my body like liquid pain. I pretty much stopped eating due to an inability to swallow. I lost thirty pounds in two months and looked like I had undergone numerous rounds of chemotherapy (minus the hair loss). I started having uncontrollable shaking throughout my body; it was so bad that it would wake me from sleep.

My Lyme disease test came back CDC positive, but this was missed by the neurologist I was seeing at the time. He wasn't even able to correctly read the results of a Western Blot Test, which is a test for Lyme disease. He kept saying that there was nothing wrong with me and he even questioned me: "What are you so afraid of?" To this day, that statement echoes in my mind more than anything any doctor has ever said to me. Was he just callous or too lazy to help me? Either way it did not reflect well on his profession. When at the age of thirty-eight, your mind abruptly stops functioning, never mind all the other physical symptoms, anyone would be scared out of their mind as to the cause. And here is this doctor pretty much telling me that it's all in my head.

I didn't dwell that much on it at the time because my symptoms became so bad so quickly that all my energy was spent on daily functions that most people take for granted. I would spend days in bed without the energy to even take a shower. The pain in my head intensified and along with it came a horrible pressure, like my head was in a vice. I was so dizzy that I frequently had to hold onto something to keep myself upright. During this time, I spoke to a friend who was diagnosed with severe, late-stage Lyme disease, and she guided me to doctors who were Lyme literate. I saw a remarkable neuro-ophthalmologist who diagnosed me with Lyme disease, Anaplasma, and Bartonella through blood tests. He was so kind and understanding and I believed that now that I had a clear diagnosis. I would begin treatment and I would soon get well – or so I thought. In this doctor's specialty, though, he did not treat Lyme disease, he only diagnosed. He referred me to a well-respected neurologist who did treat Lyme disease and co-infections. That neurologist did send me to have a SPECT scan of my brain, which measures the functioning of the brain. My results came back with severe hypoperfusion – decreased blood flow to the brain – on my right temporal lobe, which is usually consistent with neurological Lyme disease. The symptoms were real, emanating from my head LITERALLY – they were not imaginary like that other doctor insinuated. My brain was not functioning correctly and the brain scan was physical proof of this.

My mother drove me the two hours to see the specialist and I left with a prescription for a heavy dose of oral antibiotics. He told me that with Lyme disease, once the brain and nervous system are affected, IV antibiotics are usually prescribed because they are often needed in very high and constantly delivered doses in order to cross the blood-brain barrier to be able to attack the bacteria. In other words, oral antibiotics, according to many experts, are no longer effective. However, he also told me that insurance companies rarely cover the IV antibiotics. I would end up learning this the hard way just one month later.

I stayed on those oral antibiotics for a month with no relief at all. I continued to deteriorate. My ability to think and comprehend statements was being severely compromised. My fatigue was crushing. I had shooting, stabbing pain running through my brain. I continued with this new protocol for a month without any improvement. I had developed severe diarrhea from the antibiotics and my throat was covered in white spots, a sign of systemic Candida. My doctor at the time had not advised me to start probiotics, but I knew I needed them to repopulate the good bacteria that the antibiotics had killed. For a week I tried to contact my doctor without any response. I finally was able to speak with him seven days later about the side effects of the antibiotics. He was not able to offer me much guidance and I knew then that I had to find a new doctor.

Through a referral from a friend, I went to see a well-known Lyme literate doctor. My appointment lasted for two hours. I was listened to and I finally felt like someone understood me. He said I was the poster child for Lyme disease and that I was very sick. I had about sixty-five of the seventy or so symptoms associated with the disease. I was also diagnosed with Babesia, which is very common blood-borne parasite; it accompanies Lyme frequently. He told me I would need IV antibiotics (#2 Rocephin, #3 Flagyl) because the disease had progressed to the brain and nervous system . I would have to have a PICC line surgically implanted in my arm for the foreseeable future. I was also prescribed oral antibiotics to cover infections that the IV would not. I was given a long list of supplements to help support my body during this ordeal.

The journey home from the doctors was one of the worst experiences of my life. Yes, I had a plan of action and hopefully would get well, but all I could think about was the cost of this treatment. I had been doing some research on this disease when I was physically able to and the thing that always came up was the frequent denial of payment for IV medication and the required nursing by the insurance companies. If brain or nervous system involvement could be proven (usually through a spinal tap or other invasive test) a mere thirty days was all that was usually paid for. (The hospital where my spinal tap was performed only tested the spinal fluid for meningitis. When I saw my Lyme doctor afterwards, he had suggested that the spinal fluid be tested for Lyme disease. I contacted the hospital but they no longer kept my record after 15 days.) My doctor had told me that a minimum of three months would be necessary. Each month of treatment would cost about $3000, with a grand total of $9000 for all three months. I prayed that somehow this would be covered.

Since my new Lyme doctor was out of state, IV prescriptions sometimes didn't easily transfer. I found a very caring in-state general practitioner who was willing to work with my Lyme doctor. I went to see her immediately afterwards and she was able to get the first six weeks of my IV covered through insurance after spending over forty-five minutes on the phone with them while I was sitting there. I started crying when she hung up because I was so relieved. She said that I needed to start the antibiotics as soon as possible because my health was deteriorating rapidly.

The night before my PICC line was to be inserted, I was overwhelmed with emotions. I was so sick that I could never live this way, but I was afraid of putting so many drugs into my body. I was worried about the financial cost and its impact on our lives. I was increasingly worried about my children who were living with a very sick mother. But thinking that this was the most effective protocol prescribed for these infections, I knew that I had to do it. My body would have to cope somehow.

My PICC line was put in the next day and I received my first infusion of antibiotics. A visiting nurse was at my home to show me how to properly infuse so I would be able to complete this myself. Weekly nursing visits would ensue to change my PICC line dressing and monitor my vital signs.

During the next six weeks, some of my worst head symptoms began to dissipate. I always had the same three symptoms in my head: severe pain, dizziness, and pressure. Now, it was down to severe pain and dizziness. The two symptoms varied in intensity, but at least I felt like I was making a little progress. I was able to do little things like take a shower or make a very minimal dinner. I just needed more time to get well, or so I thought.

After four months of IV antibiotics, I was finally ready to have my PICC line pulled. I was so excited to be done with the grueling ordeal that accompanies having a foreign object attached to you and the limitations it presented, like taking a shower and not lifting things. I was somewhat hesitant, though, because I was nowhere near like my old self. I still had foggy head symptoms, headaches, numbness, painful eyes, and many other symptoms. I thought at the end of this treatment I would feel like my old self.

If I had known then that this journey – or should I say nightmare – had only just begun, I don't think I could have handled it.

After consultation with my Lyme literate medical doctor – or "LLMD" – I went off antibiotics . Slowly, every symptom that went away seemed to creep back. I tried many new oral antibiotics (#4 Rifampin , #5 Zithromax, #6 Minocycline) but things just kept getting worse. My head symptoms (pain, severe pressure, extreme dizziness, cognition issues) were always the worst for me but now they had a psychological component to them. I would be fine one moment and then burst out crying the next. I was developing severe depression, something I had never experienced in my life. Despair was a word I had heard people use before, but now I felt like I truly knew what it meant. Everything was snowballing.

For the next four months I was prescribed Bicillin shots. Bicillin (now up to 7 prescription drugs) is a very strong, long lasting Penicillin that is administered by means of an intramuscular shot in the buttocks. It is a white viscous liquid that hurts immensely when administered. My LLMD said some people were getting better with this and since it bypassed the stomach and went immediately into the bloodstream he told me he thought it would work better for me. I had constant stomach issues now both from the bacteria involved and the numerous pharmaceuticals I was taking.

Instead of getting better or holding steady, my health was now rapidly declining. I didn't know where to look for help. My doctor was supposed to be one of the top doctors but I wasn't getting better. I went to see another well-known Lyme doctor for a second opinion and came out feeling even worse. I had blood tests taken two weeks prior to my appointment and had even more diseases diagnosed: Epstein Barr and Chlamydia Pneumoniae were added to the list that included Lyme, Bartonella, Ehrlichia, Rickettsia, and Babesia. My white blood cell count was extremely low and I was now anemic. The doctor pretty much confirmed that I was doing everything I could to become better with my current protocol. The bacteria are very stealthy and insidious; they can evade antibiotics very easily. The number of medications I was on was a testament to that.

Pain was something now that never eluded me. My head was in constant pain. A vice-like pressure accompanied the almost daily migraine pain along with constant dizziness. I sought the help of a top East Coast hospital headache clinic – but to no avail. Every joint in my body was in agony. The pain in my ankles and wrists felt like there was a giant nail being driven through them. My feet hurt so much that walking or standing for even a couple minutes was excruciating. Keeping my eyes open due to the extreme light sensitivity and pain was unbearable. I was prescribed Tramadol, Oxycodone, Darvon, Opana, and Fioricet (we are now up to 12). These heavy duty medications didn't even touch the pain in my head.

In retrospect, I should have been more worried about the impact of these drugs on my body. I should have been more terrified about the prospect of long-term side effects. I should have more critically questioned mixing all of these prescription drugs in my body. But after a while, you just get so sick that you do not challenge the system like you should. But it was all a snowball spiraling into an avalanche that was consuming me. One drug caused something else to happen to my body, which required another drug to be prescribed, which meant I took another and another.

I then went on to Fentanyl patches (#13). These patches are one hundred times more powerful than Morphine. I was unfortunately already familiar with Fentanyl: during this time, my father was dying from Multiple Myleoma, which is an extremely painful cancer. Unbelievably, I was on the same dosage of Fentanyl as him – and it STILL did not take the pain away completely! How could that be possible? There were many nights that I wished that I would never wake up just to be out of agony. This pain stayed with me for the next three years, the worst years of my life.

My LLMD thought that since most of my gains were made on IV antibiotics I should again start using them. I was scheduled for a Hickman catheter to be surgically placed in my chest. This decision was made after I had three different PICC lines placed in my arms and they all clotted within a two-week time frame. Numerous trips to different hematologists found nothing wrong with my blood due to clotting factors. I would later find out that most people with Lyme disease and tick-borne infections have what is known as "sticky blood" which can cause clotting. I was prescribed IV Doxycycline , IV Flagyl, and IV Rifampin for the next four months. Things were not improving as they did during the first round of my IV medications. My pain would not subside and my stomach was in shambles – and so was my life. I could not enjoy any simple pleasures with my family. I know my husband and children needed more than the shell of the person I had become.

After my visit to my LLMD in September of 2010, I went on my final round of IV antibiotics. IV Tygacil (#14) was prescribed for my unrelenting symptoms. My doctor did not know why my symptoms were only continuing to get worse. This last drug was my final chance at getting well. It is one of the most powerful hospital IV drugs used. I fell apart during this time. I was barely able to eat and lost another ten pounds. I was using Protonix, Diflucan, Zomig (prescriptions 15 through 17) and probiotics to help control the stomach pain. I was using IV Glutathione (up to 18) and IV nutritional bags to help support my body to detox.

Crushing depression and anxiety were with me all the time. I felt like I was at the bottom of a well and there was no way out. It was the darkest period of my life. I would cry for days with an unrelenting sadness that I wish no one would ever experience. The all-encompassing pain coupled with the depression was numbing. I remember just laying on my bed praying over and over for this to subside. If something didn't change, I wasn't going to make it. I was prescribed Lexapro (#19) and Wellbutrin (#20) to help with the depression, Klonopin (#21) for the anxiety and severe head pressure, and multiple sleeping pills to combat the ever-present insomnia. I was a walking zombie. I envied people who could go about daily life activities: driving children to the orthodontist, going to the gym, looking over produce in the supermarket.

During this time period I sought out a doctor who

specialized in Chinese medicine and alternative therapies. I now knew that all these medications I was prescribed were not the answer. No one could live like this. I tried acupuncture, and laser and neural therapy. After not much success, I then tried bee venom therapy, ozone therapy, homeopathic medicines, and months of Heparin shots (#22). My doctor thought parasites could be a major problem for me so I went on the anti-parasitics Alinia and Biltricide. (Count it: 24 drugs!) I tried all these therapies for the next year and a half. It was not working.

My body was starting to shut down. I could not eat or sleep. My symptoms were at their absolute worst: complete exhaustion, body chills, air hunger, eye pain, horrible migraines, uncontrollable shaking, severe cognition and memory loss, drenching night sweats, extreme muscle and bone pain, bladder pain and urgency, and facial pain. I was lost, hopeless. I was bedridden. During my last visit to my LLMD he told me there was nothing left he could do for me.

My family was doing everything they could to help me through my suffering. My husband started cooking meals and doing all the shopping. My kids helped to clean the house and do the laundry. My mom would come and stay with me for days at a time and help out tremendously with the house and kids. I was so lucky to have this support. It is one thing to help out for weeks or even months during one's illness, but this was becoming years. The support from my loved ones never wavered. I am truly blessed in this respect. But with the feeling of being blessed came sadness and guilt that what my family was going through was because of me. The carnage of Lyme disease impacts everyone.

A month prior to my last LLMD visit, I had attended a local Lyme support group meeting. I had met some amazing people there and decided to contact them. I remember vividly the second meeting I had with them at a local coffee shop. After telling them that I was again scheduled for my second port placement for yet another round of IV antibiotics, they were adamant that I not go ahead with this. While talking with them, I could barely speak or comprehend all that they were saying. They told me that I needed to give my body a rest from the drugs and suggested that I see some doctors who they used to help support the body and detox. They were able to get an appointment for me the following day with a holistic doctor who I still see to this day.

After my appointment with this new doctor, I actually felt a slight flickering of hope. I had not known this feeling for so many years and thought that maybe this was the answer. I knew, though, that it would take many years. It was over four years since this journey began, and I knew at this point that getting better was not a quick fix.

There was one woman in particular who was instrumental to me in regaining my health. She introduced me to frequency therapy. While most people are afraid of experimenting with a non-FDA approved modality that virtually no one knows much about, I was more scared that if it did not work I would die. This was my last hope. Besides, there are so many things that people take and do that are not sanctioned – like supplements from health food stories – that I knew I had to reach beyond conventional medicine. Conventional medicine had its chance – four year's worth. And I was worse.

I started "rifing" in January of 2012. I started off extremely slowly and was only able to tolerate minutes at a time using the machine. I knew now that all those years of antibiotics were not at all helpful to me. My body was loaded with bacteria, which I found out due to the short amounts of time I was able to rife. After my first ten-minute treatment, I was in bed for two days with a Herxheimer healing response.

While this may sound scary – like I was stepping even further backwards – I was desperate. I knew this was a die-off reaction, and it was horrible. I had shooting pain throughout my body, unrelenting ear pain, and a massive migraine. This lasted for about a week. But the reactions went away, and then I felt like I had actually taken a step forward.

I tried to rife once a week for about fifteen minutes, gradually building up. Every herx I had after a rife session would be similar and different at the same time. It always included some kind of head pain with pressure and dizziness. My eyes, ears, and sinuses filled with pain, but this would not happen regularly. Sometimes it would be more apparent in my eyes, while other times my sinuses and ears were affected more. Migratory pain would be in my hips, knees, and pelvis. Nerve pain would affect me many times at night which made falling asleep very difficult. Also, insomnia was now a major problem for me since I had weaned off my sleeping medications.

I persisted. In spite of this pain, I was finally getting better. It felt like I was healing from the inside out. Not so much controlling symptoms, but building core strength and lowering my bacterial load.

After reading more about rife, I learned that your body goes through something called retracing. Retracing is when your body will go through all the previous symptoms you had in an illness, but in reverse order. For example, if you started off with knee pain then that symptom would probably be the last symptom to go. Now, of course, it doesn't always work like this, but it seemed to be pretty true for me and my symptoms. Also, while you are treating, you peel down the levels of disease as you would peel an onion. You have to be patient and be able to move slowly through this process.

Some people say during a crisis that either your faith becomes stronger or falls away completely. In my case, religion and praying were integral to my survival. I would pray constantly, especially when it looked like things couldn't get any worse. Every day I would pray for strength and courage and that somehow today would be a better day. On the worst of days, I would pray just to get through to the next hour. I tried to think of one positive thing a day that I was grateful for. I knew someone was listening, because slowly, very slowly, I was coming out of this nightmare.

During my first year of rifing, I also made the decision to start to wean myself off the long list of medications I was placed on during the first four years of treatment, which didn't even include antibiotics. I made a list of the medications and started very slowly with one at a time, tapering down extremely slowly. These were not medications that you could just stop taking. They all had to be tapered down. As was my experience in the past with tapering medications, my body took a long time to adjust to even a slight adjustment in dosage. This process was going to take a very long time. Along with the herxes, this was going to be a big adjustment for my body.

I would choose a drug to taper and then cut it into fourths. I began like this with all my prescriptions. Sometimes the effects of tapering were minimal, but for the most part it was incredibly hard. It would usually take at least a month for my body to acclimate to this new dosage. My head would get incredibly fuzzy; sometimes I would be extremely irritable. My brain would physically hurt. Any kind of thinking or decision making would cause my brain to become so painful, almost like it was going to explode. Many times the pain would be manifested as horrible stomach pains that would last for weeks. The gut and the brain are linked so it made sense that when tapering down drugs which affected the brain; the stomach would be involved. Sometimes, I thought I would never be rid of all these drugs at this rate. But through my sheer determination, I never once went back up on my doses. If things got really bad, I would just let my body adjust and maybe during the next cut, go a little slower. I relied on my holistic doctor greatly during that period. He forever had me immersed in Epsom salt baths to help draw the toxins out. I mean boatloads and truckloads of Epsom salts. Sometimes up to fifteen pounds at a time. Seriously.

This first year of rifing and tapering down my medications was pure hell. My pain was no longer subdued by prescriptions and the intensity of it was brutal. Even though I was not completely off all my pain prescriptions, the significant reduction was very difficult. Between that and my herxes, I spent a lot of my first year in bed. I was able to get up to shower and maybe do a couple of things around the house, and then I would have to lie down for at least a couple of hours in the afternoon. On good days, I would be able to make dinner and stay up for an hour or two after dinner. Before I had gotten sick, I was an avid exerciser. Now, a short walk would make my head hurt badly and I would become extremely dizzy. I tried to walk a little every day because I knew it was good for me. It helped to push out the toxins and get things moving. I made it a point to try and walk at least five times a week if possible. Then I started to go to the pool as well. Progress. I was making progress. Slowly. But sometimes I questioned it.

During this time my emotions along with my body were on a rollercoaster. Not just due to the infection in my brain and body, but not really knowing if this new plan was going to succeed. After a lifetime of relying on the medical community to know the best way to treat a disease, I was mostly on my own. (Aside from the small rifing community, which was amazing.) The traditional medical community had failed me. They did not have answers for me anymore, which led me to find my own path to wellness. I was filled with anger at times, and at other times immense sadness. Was I getting better? Would I make it out of my Lyme inferno? Many days, I did not think I could go on, but with sheer determination, outright stubbornness, my holistic practitioner, and my amazing family and friends, I plowed on.

During the second year of rifing, I also tried other modalities to support my body and immune system. I veered away from traditional Western medicine and explored more holistic methods. I couldn't put any more meds into my system. I wanted to find doctors who treated by other means besides prescriptions. I used chiropractors, cranial sacral work, infrared sauna, bodywork, and acupuncture. Through my friends, I had found some wonderful doctors and therapists to help my body overcome this horrific ordeal.

I was slowly coming out of a very long nightmare. I had glimpses of my former self that would propel me forward when things got tough. This new regimen was working for me. My friends and family would comment on my progress; "Wow, you really look better. You seem to have so much more energy." It was reassuring to hear such positive feedback. It made me even more determined to succeed. I could manage more household chores, more activities. I remember the day I went to my first spinning class in over five years. I started to cry with joy.

I still experienced bad herxes from my rifing sessions, but I was able to control and predict my symptoms much better. If I knew that I had a certain appointment or event that I had to attend, I would make sure that I didn't rife or incorporate any treatment session for four days prior. Usually, this would work, and I felt I was somewhat participating in life again. After such a long time of relentless sickness and symptoms, it was a great feeling. My local physician that was still monitoring me from time to time, and helping me wean off pharmaceuticals, was even shocked when my blood work looked normal for the first time in years.

I am currently in my fourth year of rifing and I am completely off all my prescriptions. I see a holistic doctor every two weeks to continue to help strengthen my body. I am able to exercise at the level I was at previously. I try to eat very well and limit stress in my life. I am still not able to work full-time but I know that eventually I will get there. What I do most mornings before 10:30am is more than what I used to be able to do in one week.

My children have a full-time mother again, my husband has his wife back, and my amazing mother has a much healthier daughter back. I have rejoined the land of the living. Last summer, I was even able to ride bikes with the kids at the shore. I went with my family and my mother on a vacation to Europe. I have learned how to laugh and smile again.

I look at life in an entirely different manner now. I try to enjoy every moment in the now because I now know how things can change so drastically. I am a much more empathetic person because you really never know truly how others are doing. Just because someone looks healthy to you doesn't mean they aren't suffering inside. I try and help as many people as I can who are going through this horrible disease because I know firsthand how scary and isolating it can be.

If I could take one thing away from my journey of escaping the Lyme inferno, it would be to always trust yourself. Only you know your body and what feels right to you. If something isn't working for you, after a fair amount of time put into it, change things up. People must look for their own answers especially in diseases where the medical community has such differing opinions. No one has all the answers, as many people would like to believe. You have to be willing and able to search out different and diverse methods of healing which can be extremely challenging if you are very ill. You must continually search for the right mix which resonates with you and makes you feel alive again.

CALL ME JASON

In my family, I was one of the lucky ones who was not sick. To this day, I cannot relate to a daily war of physical anguish and mental anxiety. I can only begin to imagine the suffering my mother endured because I watched so much of it unfold right before my own eyes. She was healthy and vivacious, and then in a matter of weeks, bed-ridden and in endless pain. She went to twenty different physicians and specialists, and she received almost as many diagnoses; those who could not name an illness simply shrugged their shoulders or claimed it was "all in her head."

I cannot begin to imagine what would have happened to my mother and my family if she had not ultimately figured out that the root of all her debilitating and painful symptoms was Lyme disease. I would have seen my mother as a medical tragedy or a psychological loony bird. I would have never questioned the pervasive sickness and pain in so many other people – in my family, my community, and society as a whole.

I wish this single encounter with Lyme disease was enough to enlighten me. But it took me years to truly understand what my mother had endured for so many years. More than years, it took me hearing and witnessing the stories of others – stories that ran almost exactly parallel to the stories of my own family. Stories like those of Sage and Alexandra and Mike and Ann and James.

Sometimes, a mirror reflection can offer a clearer picture than reality.

It hit a point when the number of anecdotal cases of suffering I encountered hit a critical mass. My brain could no longer disregard the endless stream of inexplicable ailments and mystifying misdiagnoses. There were too many sick people – physically and mentally – and too many prescriptions. There were too many chronically ill boys and girls, young mothers and fathers resigned to daily neurological horrors of ADHD, MS, and Parkinson's. There were too many people with something that the doctors could not figure out. Or the doctors had "figured it out" and assigned a name to the confounding set of symptoms, but there was never a cure beyond lifestyle and dietary restrictions and a daily regimen of medication – never any hope for permanent resolution.

Only after encountering so many other stories did I start to see the world differently.

I was raised just like millions of others in this country to not question the medical system. They were the experts. They had the training.

I also grew up with a loving mother. She was fun and devoted – and healthy. As a kid, you take your parent's health for granted. You just assume every morning that your mom and dad are already awake, functioning perfectly normally. The fragility of health is a shattering realization for any child. It is scary and frustrating to watch your parents suffer no matter how old you are. But when you are young – when your parents are not supposed to be sick – it is a lot tougher.

Needless to say, when my mother got sick and nobody knew what was wrong with her, I gave her love, but definitely not the support she needed. She had no diagnosis. Her pain was invisible to me and the rest of us. It was only apparent through her rants and torrents of tears. Her uplifting demeanor was replaced by utter despair. Lyme disease is not like cancer where patients undergoing chemo lose their hair. It can be impossible to see, and as a result impossible to understand.

It is cruel that a disease that can inflict so much damage can be so well masked. It is cruel that so many people who have Lyme disease appear like they are functioning normally that others assume they are healthy. It is cruel that Lyme disease and a laundry list of co-infections so often mimic other ailments that people do not realize what is actually afflicting their bodies. It is truly insidious.

So I loved my mom, but to be honest, I thought she had lost her marbles a bit. We all did. She was completely uncorked. What can be most likened to nervous breakdowns were an all too regular occurrence in our household. This misguided notion clouded my judgment. It delayed my enlightenment far too long.

When I left for college, living away from the ground zero that my home had become, it became easier to ignore and dismiss my mom's reality. I was even slightly relieved. Even now, though, I doubt it would have been any better if I was still living at home like the rest of my family. I would not have been much help. I would have been another person rolling their eyes and gritting their teeth every time my mother's anxiety overcame the household.

I would have been too consumed surviving my mom's survival. It would have been impossible for me to take the step back that I needed to see the bigger picture: that my mom was far from the only person suffering such a fate – that my family was more typical than we all realized.

Fortunately, my family was different in one key way: how my mom handled her illness. She did not settle for a tragic death sentence even when some doctor suggested she had early-stage MS. She – in spite of her most intense anxieties – looked in the mirror day after day seeking answers based in logic and reason – some rationale to explain the interconnectivity of her myriad of symptoms.

She saw so many doctors that she had her introduction practically memorized: *I am a woman who is not even fifty. I have never been sick before in my life. Within two months, I have seen nearly twenty doctors. Can you please help me?*

So she advocated for herself in a way that no physician was willing to do. Physicians embraced the diagnoses they assigned – even when they lacked reason or hope. They were used to their patients embracing these diagnoses in turn. No physician appeared to be accustomed to a patient who was unwilling to accept the fate assigned to her by someone with the initials MD at the end of their name. Yet, my mother's dogged determination to defy the medical authorities only seemed to validate their arguments that she was a "head case." It took me too long to realize who was actually the head case.

Ultimately, my mom diagnosed herself, and later had it confirmed by several physicians. When one treatment after another did not work, she sought out new ways to restore her health. Her battle took years, but she finally feels that she is physically healthy enough to live a full life. The trauma from enduring such a test to her sanity and willpower are scars permanently ingrained into her being. She has post-traumatic stress about medical tests to this day. Even when she goes for her routine annual mammogram, she enters the office shaking like a dog going to the kennel.

But my mom's journey to restoring her health is only a small part of my point. Because even as she was getting healthier – even as I witnessed with my own eyes various modes of unconventional healing seemingly working – I still needed to look beyond my own family's story to understand the bigger picture.

In the state in which I currently live, an organization publishes a booklet on Lyme disease. A checklist of nearly 200 symptoms covers six pages.

It oftentimes begins with a circular rash – the standard indicator for a Lyme diagnosis, even though the bull's eye rash occurs in less than half of Lyme patients. Needless to say, this rash is not intended to be solely used in clinical diagnosis, yet many physicians will still dismiss the very mention of Lyme disease without a visible rash.

The booklet's checklist continues beyond the rash and flulike symptoms to cover an astounding array of categories – from Musculoskeletal to Neurological to Psychological Well-Being.

During her initial years of self-conducted Lyme disease treatment, my mother introduced me to dozens of people whose paths she crossed. Their stories were all the same. These were people equally desperate in their daily anguished nightmares. It was a cruel 'mad lib' replicated over and over again, only with different names and symptoms.

Why had it taken me so long to see this pattern? In my current line of work, I frequently work with families. I joke with parents that if teenagers listened to their moms and dads the first, fifth, or fiftieth time, I would be out of a job very quickly. When you are too close to something, reality and reason are oftentimes more difficult to accept and achieve. I was too close to my mother's story, to her suffering.

I am ashamed to admit it, but, in retrospect, I truly believe the fundamental difference came in how a person conveyed their battle with Lyme disease to me. When other people share their stories, there was no yelling or screaming. There was clearly anger and resentment and anxiety, but there was a calm collectedness in their retellings. There was a blunt presentation of facts.

Of course, meeting someone once and hearing their story is a lot different than living with someone and living their nightmare. I was lost in my mother's wailing. It was like a thick fog in the night, blinding my vision. Enduring the same hysterics on a day in, day out basis made it nearly impossible to actually hear the words she was saying and have true sympathy and understanding.

Only when I met so many others like my mother did it all make sense in a way it never had before – in a way it should have so much earlier. I had not seen the forest through the trees. But now there were trees everywhere – mothers and fathers, sons and daughters, all with stories that echoed the same words and experiences.

In an episode of one of my favorite television shows, How I Met Your Mother, the characters examine each other's "buts" – the things about other people that once you notice them, you can never stop noticing them. In the show, these "buts" were likened to annoying habits like loud chewing or always grammatically correcting other people. For me, the more I met with people and families who shared with me their Lyme disease battles, the more I was realizing a terrible "but" about the world around me. And it has been isolating ever since.

I saw people around me in a new light. They all seemed happy and healthy, but a shocking number of my peers – all in their late teens and early twenties, coming from a diversity of religions, nationalities, and ethnicities – had bizarre medical histories, anomalies that I would never before have questioned. There was one guy in my fraternity whose hands had uncontrollable tremors – difficult to see with the naked eye, but significant enough that he could never pursue his dreams of having a career as a surgeon. Another guy I knew suffered from intense, debilitating bouts of migraines; by the time I met him they had gone on for years. He had been to at least twenty different doctors and none of them had any explanation for his condition – let alone a diagnosis or any way to offer lasting relief. There were too many girls to count on the birth control pill, not to prevent a pregnancy, but because they had an array of other medical issues the pill was supposed to camouflage. I often wondered what would happen to them when they finally went off the pill to start a family.

Now in my job, I rarely encounter a completely healthy family. I know that sounds dramatic. I know that sounds improbable. But with a sample size of hundreds of families, through an objective statistical analysis, I know what I am witnessing is more the norm than the exception.

I am not saying that every family has someone on life support or with a terminal illness. I am not saying every family has someone with a serious mental illness or physical disability. But let's just say that nearly every family I have encountered is 'unwell' in some way or ways.

Nearly every family has something. They are healthy – "BUT" … and then I get a story. The children have IEPs (Individualized Educational Programs), which are assigned based on learning differences, difficulties, and disabilities. They have allergies, intolerances, conditions, tendencies, anxieties, and any number of limitations. There are prescriptions, daily medications family members must take just to make it through the day. The diagnoses I hear on a daily basis run an astounding gamut. The majority of people I encounter have no cure, just prescription drugs they rely on day in and day out.

I do not understand why so many people simply accept this fate, and why so few people insist on digging deeper to be truly healthy. To rid themselves of any medications. To no longer have any diseases attached to their identity.

In a way, all of this is as much an indictment of us as patients as it is on the physicians. Why do we not ask more questions? Why do we not push back when we are told there is no answer, or when we are given an answer that proves unsatisfactory, or when we are given an answer that is terminal? Maybe then the stories of Sage and Alexandra and Mike and Ann and James would be the rule, not the exception.

As for the physicians, undoubtedly there would be many who would condescend and rebuke any notion that they are wrong. But I believe there are hidden heroes out there – doctors who need to read the stories in this book, to reevaluate how they look at patients. Maybe one of them will help to create real change for the vast community of people suffering from Lyme disease and other tick-borne infections – or at the very least save even one more life.

Talking about health – especially the lack thereof – can be very difficult. It is a personal, sensitive, and touchy subject. People do not like to think about themselves as being unhealthy. The mere suggestion that they are in any way unwell can elicit a rude and dismissive response. "I'm fine! Stop bothering me! You're being ridiculous!"

I am scarred from watching my mother try to help some of her friends who she saw were suffering. Even the suggestion that they get tested for Lyme disease evoked some nasty responses. Some people, instead of expressing gratitude that their friend was trying to look out for them, stopped talking to my mother completely. They thought she had lost her mind. They didn't want to deal with her. Now, through the grapevines, I know that many of them are dealing with things a lot worse than my mother's prodding: MS, Parkinson's, fibromyalgia, debilitating migraines. They are not old people – many initially started experiencing symptoms in their 40s and 50s, far too young by most anyone's standards for these serious ailments. And they are suffering.

There are very few people outside of my family who I have confided in regarding my observations and sentiments. Even these conversations never get far. They either do not understand, or claim they understand but have nothing to offer other than a listening ear. It's better than being dismissed.

So I am left nervous, hesitant to say anything. Because even if I say something and they do listen, then they need a positive Lyme disease test. These tests are wholly unreliable – and even when they come back positive, far too many physicians dismiss the results as false-positives or insist it must be something else.

But then, even if they get a positive diagnosis and know they have Lyme disease, the recovery is long. Escaping the inferno of Lyme disease, as Sage and Alexandra and Mike and Ann and James have established in this collection of memoirs, is an arduous journey. It requires nearly limitless love, support, guidance, money, time, energy, and persistence. Fighting to restore normalcy to your health – or even a semblance of normalcy – can take years.

But that fight should be worth it! The alternative is years of suffering, so why not suffer towards a solution rather than certain doom?

That is why I am writing this chapter now – to provide some encouragement, hope, and wisdom to those who have family members and loved one who are sick from Lyme disease, or are simply sick from something that no one can firmly diagnose. I want to be the 'other person' – the person outside of your home and your daily life – whose story can provide insight and comfort.

There is a story in Judaism that the Lord did not simply part the Red Sea for Moses and the Jews as they fled from Egypt. This story says that there was a common man who waded into the water until he was neck-deep. Only then did the Lord part the waters for the exodus.

The moral? We cannot wait for others to part the waters in front of us so we can have sanctuary and freedom from suffering. We must take the first step. We are responsible for our fate.

I love this story and its moral. Especially when I think about the people in this book. I admire them all and the thousands of others like them who took that first step and have fought so hard for themselves. They are inspiring...

But again – should they be so inspiring? Should this not be a human instinct – to advocate for yourself at all costs? Why is an insistence on personal health not automatic? Why do so many people just accept their diagnoses?

In studying writing, I was trained to reveal narratives in the world around me. In the case of Lyme disease, there is little left for inference or investigation. A person with a previously perfect bill of health is suddenly debilitated by a collection of seemingly unrelated symptoms that all start around the same time for no apparent reason. Said person visits numerous medical professionals and experts to get a diagnosis and a cure. Most medical professionals trained in traditional Western medicine have no insights or any idea; they have no diagnosis and no cure. Those that claim to have an answer rarely offer a long-term solution or hope.

Countless blood tests are run. Lyme is mostly dismissed, if it is even ever considered.

This brings me to the most infuriating rhetorical question of all: why, if a medical practitioner can provide no answer and no hope for a patient, would they not consider just one more illness, one more blood test? How come so many doctors do their due diligence for so many other arbitrary ailments but negligently, and sometimes defiantly, object to any possibility that it can by Lyme disease?

There are rational – even if I do not deem them acceptable – answers to this question: medical guidelines have dismissed the reality of "chronic Lyme disease," thus minimizing the destructiveness of the disease. No laboratory has devised a foolproof test for Lyme disease. Furthermore, top medical authorities insist on perpetuating the myths of a bulls-eye rash and two weeks of antibiotic treatment.

There is also the fact that so many people who do have Lyme disease sound like raving lunatics when they speak with healthy (or seemingly "healthy") people. Unlike cancer or heart disease, Lyme is stealth, in turn yielding no sympathy from the average person. The apathy, irritation, and anger that ensues from an inability to understand only incites more desperation, hysteria, and anxiety from Lyme sufferers. Ultimately, dialogues are terminated, relationships are ruined, and families are fractured – sometimes irreconcilably. The stigma surrounding Lyme disease is so toxic that people will not even entertain it as part of the consideration.

I saw the damage Lyme disease inflicted on my family in this way. The Lyme inferno engulfed not only my mother, but our entire family. It caused years of tension, stress, anxiety, and sadness – years that are impossible to get back.

I spent years waking up every morning – at home or hundreds of miles away at college – wondering how my mother would be suffering that day. It was like a portion of my mind and an unrelenting pit in my stomach were constantly devoted to worrying about what each day would bring to her, and in turn my family. When my mother regained most of her health, I cannot tell you how liberating it was for me to not have to stress out every time her number popped up on my cell phone or every time I saw her. Lyme disease is volatile, and the anxiety it induces afflicts everyone in a family. Every day is unpredictable, which makes every day unpredictable for the entire family.

Fortunately, for my family, the damage was not completely irreparable. Fortunately, discovering truths and developing a deeper understanding of the enemy brought us all closer together. It allowed us to more deeply respect one another – especially my mother, who turned out to be anything but a head case. Her clarity was her saving grace.

Sometimes, I imagine myself as a doctor. If a patient came to me for care, and I could not provide that care – let alone any insights into why they needed that care in the first place – I would be desperate to find that person an answer.

Intellectually, I would want to understand what was wrong with my patient.

Humanely, I would want to restore that patient's health.

Egotistically, I would not want to come across as clueless.

Why are doctors not listening? I understand that no doctor wants to hear the Lyme community lambast Western medicine and launch tirades against the medical profession. But – and I could say this as someone from any line of work – if I do not have the answer to a client's questions, or if I have failed to help them, then I am bothered by the fact that I have not done my job adequately. I feel personally accountable for that person's diagnosis and recovery, for that family's peace of mind. I feel like I have let them down, and I try even harder than ever to bring them answers and hope.

This is a plea to the disbelieving and disregarding, to those of you who dismiss the pain and fury of those who have been dismissed all too often. Listen to these stories. Listen to the stories around you.

If someone you love has unexplained symptoms, if someone you love is being told they are crazy – even when they are acting crazy – they just might need a person who cares enough to help encourage them to challenge their status quo, to question the system. You can be that person. You can be the turning point in their lives, the inspiration and insight to begin down a road to recovery.

If you speak up, then maybe that person you love and the people around that person – and even you – can also escape their inferno.

Share these memoirs with others. Write your own. Speak up – for yourself and for others. Make your voice heard. If you save just one life, even if it is your own, then it is worth it.

CITATIONS

Conroy, Pat. *The Lords of Discipline*. New York: Dial Press, 2006.

O'Connor, Flannery. *Wise Blood*. New York: Farrar, Straus and Giroux, 2007.

Made in the USA
San Bernardino,
CA